THE FIRST AMERICAN SC

The First American School of Sociology

W. E. B. Du Bois and the Atlanta Sociological Laboratory

EARL WRIGHT II

University of Cincinnati, USA

Routledge
Taylor & Francis Group

LONDON AND NEW YORK

First published 2016 by Ashgate Publishing

2 Park Square, Milton Park, Abingdon, Oxfordshire OX14 4RN
711 Third Avenue, New York, NY 10017

Routledge is an imprint of the Taylor & Francis Group, an informa business

First issued in paperback 2017

British Library Cataloguing in Publication Data
A catalogue record for this book is available from the British Library.

The Library of Congress Cataloging-in-Publication Data has been applied for.

ISBN 978-1-4724-6700-3 (hbk)
ISBN 978-1-138-47677-6 (pbk)

Contents

Preface

In the fall of 1995 I entered the master's degree program in sociology at the University of Memphis at the behest of an instructor who knew that I had only taken one sociology course as an undergraduate. I was a history major and Black studies minor who only chose the master's degree program in sociology over education because of the assistantship that I received. During the first semester of my first year in graduate school I visited Elizabeth Higginbotham, the person who encouraged me to enter the program, to explain why I had decided to walk away from sociology and enter the education program. I told her that I wanted to pursue my lifelong dream of becoming a high school history teacher and head high school football coach. While it was true that my dream to that point was to teach high school history and coach high school football at my alma mater, those were not the primary reasons I decided to leave the program. I eventually stumbled my way toward disclosing my real reasons to her. As with many first year students, I doubted whether or not I was capable of competing with my classmates and able to complete the degree. This was all the more traumatizing since members of my cohort were more than willing to disclose their GRE scores and I realized that mine was the lowest of the nearly ten member group. Despite my low GRE score I was confident that I could complete the program if I put in enough time and effort. Our conversation then veered toward the real reason that I had decided to leave the program. I wanted to leave sociology because I could not envision how my passion, the study and development of strategies to assist in the uplift of Black Americans, might fit within the discipline. To this point I had read many sociology articles and books on the experiences and conditions of Blacks, but it was from a deficit perspective. I did not believe there was a place for my research interests within the discipline. By the end of my meeting with Elizabeth she had convinced me that I could, in fact, blend my interests in Black Studies and history with sociology and from a perspective that did not view Blacks as deficient actors in this society. She emphasized that much research was needed in my areas and that I could become an expert on the topic. With this reassuring information in mind I aggressively attacked my coursework and began to plan my thesis project.

When the time came to select a topic for my thesis I thought about the advice Elizabeth offered to our professional development seminar class on the selection of a thesis or dissertation topic. "Choose a topic that is meaningful and personal to you," she said. And, "start where you are." The essence of her message was clear. Engage in research that is significant and special to you since you will be dealing with the subject matter intensely for quite some time and you do not want to grow bored or uninterested with the topic. After a rather eventful day at my barbershop when a gun was wielded before the customers and me, I decided to write my thesis on the Black barbershop. During the search of the existing literature I quickly discovered a dearth of social science studies on the barbershop. I was then instructed by my thesis advisor, Carol Ronai, to expand my literature search to include an examination of urban sociology and urban communities. It was at this time that I was introduced to the many volumes of work on the, supposed, first American school of sociology: the Chicago School of Sociology. Article after article and book after book referred to the Chicago School as the architects of urban sociology while citing its numerous accomplishments that began around 1915 with the arrival of Robert Park and Ernest Burgess. As I examined this literature I became troubled by the accolades bestowed upon them. I was bothered for quite some time about the exalted status bestowed on the Chicago School but I could not understand why. Then one day while visiting my grandmother it became clear to me. As a youth I split time living between three households: my mother's home, my aunt's home and my grandparents' home. One of the reasons that I loved living with my grandparents was because they had a bookshelf filled with lots of books. It was at my grandparents' house that I remember, as a small child, being enthralled by a book with a controversial title and a funny name for the author. I was so fascinated with the title that I had already read a substantial part of this book before reaching age ten (albeit, I didn't understand ANY of what I was reading). The book with the funny title that captured my imagination as a youth was *The Philadelphia Negro* by W. E. B. Du Bois.

After rediscovering Du Bois's classic text during graduate school I fully understood my discomfort and began questioning my professors and classmates on why the Chicago School of Sociology and the Pittsburgh monographs were considered early urban sociological architects and classic studies, respectively, and not W. E. B. Du Bois and *The Philadelphia Negro* that predated both. I received no answer that sufficiently quelled my discontent. I then delved intensely into the early sociological work of Du Bois. I reasoned that if *The Philadelphia Negro* was published and was excluded from mainstream sociological recognition in 1899, then there were possibly other studies by Du Bois that were also important but unknown. I soon discovered the existence of the Atlanta University Study of the Negro Problems. This 20-volume collection of investigations so captured my attention that I was faced with a quandary. Should I continue with my thesis on the barbershop and complete the requirements for the master's degree within a few months or should I change my thesis topic to the Atlanta University studies, take an extra year to complete the MA degree and enter a doctoral program without an already established dissertation topic? The choice was simple. I completed the barbershop thesis, which resulted in two peer reviewed publications, and pursued my interest in the Atlanta University studies in my doctoral program.

I took the doctorate in 2000, under the guidance, mentorship and friendship of Thomas C. Calhoun, at the University of Nebraska. When my first series of articles on the contributions and significance of the Atlanta Sociological Laboratory were released in 2002 I expected the seas to part, sky to open and the world to excitedly, unabashedly and finally, embrace and acknowledge the contributions of W. E. B. Du Bois and the Atlanta Sociological Laboratory as seminal works within the discipline. Sadly, after nearly 15 years of waiting this earth-shattering event still has not occurred. While there are cursory acknowledgements of Atlanta University being the academic home of W. E. B. Du Bois during his years as a practicing sociologist, *no* current sociology textbook offers an articulation of the significance of the Atlanta Sociological Laboratory to the discipline. Instead there continues to be only tumultuous *silence* within the sociological community when it comes to recognizing the accomplishments of this school. It is my sincere desire that this book signals the beginning of an era of appreciation for the works of Du Bois and the many known and unknown members of the Atlanta Sociological Laboratory.

I apologize in advance for any redundancy found between chapters and for referencing the reader to my previous work on this topic. Some of the arguments or information herein have been published before in another form. Accordingly, at various points the reader is directed to specific reference points such that additional information on the topic may be found. Although it would be ideal to include an exhaustive presentation of everything that I've discovered on this topic, limitations on space prevent me from doing so. Despite this challenge, this book is significant because it is 1) the first book length treatment of a department of sociology at a predominately Black institution; 2) the first book length treatment of the entire methodological techniques employed by the Du Bois-led Atlanta

Sociological Laboratory and 3) the first effort to successfully debunk the notion that the Chicago School comprised the first American school of sociology. While mainstream recognition of the greatness of this school is yet to come, I sincerely hope that this book serves as a clarion call to those committed to offering a more holistic understanding of the history of sociology in the United States to find a specific area that has been under researched, or not researched at all, and fill in the remaining gaps such that following generations will know that their journey is not new. For me, this journey of understanding the Atlanta Sociological Laboratory began in 1995 because of a book that I discovered on my grandparents' bookshelf. That bookshelf led me to pursuing what has become my life's passion. I cannot express enough gratitude to my grandparents for placing on their shelf a book authored by a man with a weird name that led me down this path. For that, and the many other wonderful things that you did for me, Grandma and Grandad, I will always love you and will always cherish your memory.

Your child, Dr. Earl "Peacock Mississippi" Wright II.

Chapter 1
From the Cotton Field to the Classroom

Africans in America were legally ensnared in the barbaric and peculiar institution of slavery for 246 years: 1619–1865. The legally sanctioned imprisonment of this group was driven largely by economic forces that viewed them as sub-human dark skinned people from the *dark continent* who were exploitable commodities valuable only as components within the development of both the American and global economies. Once enslaved, economic interests compelled some owners of kidnapped Africans to allow select chattel to obtain limited levels of education in areas directly related to their responsibilities on the plantation.[1] The prevailing view on the education of Blacks during this era was that such ambitions should be denied at all costs. One reason that Blacks in America were denied educational opportunities was the belief that "if they were educated they would read abolition papers and would be discontented" (Hunter 1922: 8). While one can surmise there was definite cause to believe that a forcibly enslaved populous would eventually become discontent with their condition, owners of enslaved Africans were more afraid that upon educating America's three-fifths of a person populous they would not be merely discontent but committed to taking up arms against those who had enslaved them. Despite allowing enslaved Africans of the American South 'oral training and that for servility' and limiting the type of education received by free Blacks in the American North, fear of slave revolts was the impetus behind the establishment of state laws prohibiting the education of Blacks in America.[2]

---

1   See R. I. Brigham. 1945. "Negro Education in Ante bellum Missouri." *The Journal of Negro History* 30(4): 405–420.

2   See C. W. Birnie. 1927. "Education of the Negro in Charleston, South Carolina, prior to the Civil War." *Journal of Negro History* 12(1): 13–21; R. I. Brigham. 1945. "Negro Education in Ante bellum Missouri." *The Journal of Negro History* 30(4): 405–420; Ronald E. Butchart and Amy F. Rolleri. 2004. "Secondary Education and Emancipation: Secondary Schools for Freed Slaves in the American South, 1862–

Laws limiting the educational opportunities available to Blacks can be traced back to 1740 when the state of South Carolina declared:

> Whereas, the having of slaves taught to write or suffering them to be employed in writing may be attended with inconveniences, be it enacted, That all and every person and persons—whatsoever, who shall hereafter teach or cause any slave or slaves to be taught, or who shall use or employ any slave as a scribe in any manner of writing whatever, hereafter to write, every such person or persons shall for every such offense forfeit the sum of $100 current money. (Du Bois 1901: 19)

In 1770 Georgia passed legislation penalizing those who taught enslaved Blacks to read or write the amount of $20. In the wake of periodic slave revolts that many owners of enslaved Africans believed were directly connected to the ability of some Blacks to read, the Georgia legislature amended its law to apply not only to the enslaved but to Whites and free Blacks as well.

> If any slave, Negro or free person of color, or any White person shall teach any other slave, Negro or free person of color to read or write, either written or printed characters, the same free person of color or slave shall be punished by fine and whipping, or fine or whipping, at the discretion of the court; and if a white person so offend, he, she, or they shall be punished with a fine not exceeding $500 and imprisonment in the common jail at the discretion of the court. (ibid.: 18)

While the criminalization of Black education is generally associated with southern and border states like Alabama, Louisiana, Missouri, North Carolina and Virginia, who passed similarly restrictive laws, the limiting of educational opportunities for free Blacks in the American North took the form of mob violence against Black schools in Connecticut, New York, Pennsylvania, Ohio and other locations.[3]

Despite state laws aimed at preventing the education of Blacks in the South and the North's tactics of violence and intimidation, there were some relatively successful attempts at educating America's second class citizens during the pre-Civil War era. Perhaps the earliest was Elias Neau's

---

1875." *Pedagogica Historica* 40: 157–181; Frances L. Hunter. 1922. "Slave Society on the Southern Plantation." *Journal of Negro History* 7(1): 1–10.

3   See W. E. B. Du Bois. 1901. *The Negro Common School.* Atlanta, GA: Atlanta University Press.

school in New York. Neau opened his school in 1704 and over the next 18 years educated more than 200 enslaved and free Blacks. Other attempts to provide educational opportunities for enslaved and free Blacks included Anthony Benezet and the Philadelphia Quakers' effort of 1770, Prince Hall's Massachusetts school of 1798 and Prudence Crandall's Ohio efforts of the 1800s. Surprisingly, the American South hosted several schools for Blacks during the pre-Civil War era. Included among these was a school in Charleston, South Carolina that opened in 1744 and lasted ten years, the St. Frances Academy that was established by the Roman Catholic Church in Maryland in 1829 and Julian Froumontaine's Savannah, Georgia school that openly educated free Blacks between 1819–1829 "and secretly sometime after."[4]

"I Will Find a Way or Make One"

President Abraham Lincoln's signing of the Emancipation Proclamation and passage of the Thirteenth Amendment to the Constitution of the United States not only signaled the end of the legalized enslavement of Blacks in America, it ended the *de jure* criminalization of education for Blacks in the nation. Prior to this period there existed in some states laws criminalizing Blacks attempting to obtain an education and, in other cases, Whites assisting Blacks in obtaining an education. The formal dissolution of these laws allowed for the much delayed formal education of Blacks. The educational opportunities available to Blacks following emancipation consisted of common school instruction in the basics of "readin', 'ritin and 'rithmatic." Common was the name given to schools where people of varying ages and grade levels were taught; generally, in the same classroom. It was not uncommon for adults and pre-teens to be classmates and receive the same instruction on elementary school skills. Usually housed in poorly built one room structures, the curriculum of the common school was consistent with contemporary elementary and middle schools. The length of the school year for students in the South, unlike their northern counterparts, was not dictated by school officials, but the farming season. If the child's labor was needed during the planting or harvesting season then their duties as a student became secondary in importance. While the common school did accomplish its primary goal of instilling basic skills and knowledge, the need for teachers to educate the millions of newly

---

4   Ibid.

freed American citizens led to the development of a different type of school. Normal schools were established, primarily, to train those who wanted to become teachers. If the curriculum of the common school can be considered consistent with contemporary elementary and middle school work, then the normal school curriculum can be considered consistent with contemporary high school and junior college work. The founding of common and normal schools was an important step in Black education and societal advancement as they provided opportunities to satisfy one's intellectual curiosity while preparing the more ambitious of the race for the challenges and possibilities of pursuing a liberal arts or vocational education at any of the many Black institutions being established during this era.

In the middle and late 1800s Americans witnessed a growth in the number of schools established across the southern and mid-Atlantic regions for the higher education of Blacks. According to William Edward Burghardt (W. E. B.) Du Bois, author of the first objective and scientific inquiry of Black higher education in America, there existed five types of schools for Blacks during this period. *Ante-bellum schools* were "established before the war and represent[ed] the abolition movement" (e.g., Lincoln University [1854] and Wilberforce University [1856] [Du Bois 1900: 12]). The second category of schools, *Freedmen's Bureau Schools*, were "established directly after the war by Missionary and Freedmen's Aid Societies under the protection and for the most part under the direct patronage of the Freedmen's Bureau" (e.g., Fisk University [1866], Atlanta University [1867] and Howard University [1867] [Du Bois 1900: 12]). *Church schools* "were established mainly by Church societies after the closing up of the Freedmen's Bureau" (e.g., Benedict College [1870], Wiley University [1873] and Knoxville College [1879] [ibid.: 13]). The fourth group consisted of *schools of Negro church bodies* "that culminated in the eighties and led to a movement to found schools among the Negro churches" (e.g., Livingstone College [1880], Morris Brown College [1885] and Paul Quinn College [1885] [ibid.: 13]). The establishment of the final group of schools, *state schools*, "was due almost entirely to the United States' statutes of 1862 and 1890 donating public lands to the several states for endowing agricultural colleges" (e.g., Virginia N & C Institute [1883], Georgia State Industrial College [1890] and Delaware State College [1891] [ibid.: 13]).

Atlanta University was "established by the American Missionary Association [and] aided by the Freedmen's Bureau" in 1867 (ibid.: 6). The Catalogue of Officers and Students of Atlanta University (1897: 43) states that the founding of Atlanta University:

Dates back to the days immediately succeeding the Civil War, when farsighted missionary teachers and officers of the Freedmen's Bureau saw the necessity of founding an institution in which opportunities for higher instruction should be afforded to colored youth, and which should be able to furnish teachers and other educated leaders to the newly emancipated race.

When Atlanta University officially opened in 1869 it became "the first educational institution of higher learning in Georgia to open its doors to all people, regardless of race, color or creed" (ibid.: 24). The school's integrationist posture on student enrollment negatively impacted the fiscal health of the institution a few years after its opening.

Upon its establishment Atlanta University, under the supervision of the state of Georgia, was overseen by the Board of Visitors who periodically toured the institution to review its daily operations and examine its fiscal dealings. A special report on the school was made by the board in 1871 and regular reports were submitted between 1874 and 1887. For the most part, reviews of the school were favorable. In the 1882 report it was written, "We do not believe that we have ever seen better teaching than we find done at the Atlanta University" (Adams 1930: 24). While the Board of Visitors mostly offered positive reviews of the school, it wasn't until 1887 that this body noticed something troubling on the campus.

In 1887 the visitors noticed what had apparently not been especially observed by them before that time, that white children were attending the institution … As a matter of fact what had happened was, that it was convenient for the children of the teachers to attend the institution. That same was also true of the children of a white missionary who was in charge of a colored church in the city, and who was sympathetically but not officially connected with Atlanta University. (ibid.: 24–25)

Given the racial sensibilities of White Georgians in the 1880s, the only appropriate response to a publicly funded institution of higher education in that state that adhered to a non-discriminatory admissions policy was the creation of legislation criminalizing such actions by government funded entities. The "Glenn Bill," named after its principal architect legislature W. C. Glenn, affirmed that:

By this bill all trustees and officers and teachers of Atlanta University would become liable to punishment by a fine not to exceed one thousand dollars; or by imprisonment not to exceed six months; or by sentence to work in a chain gang on the public works not to exceed twelve months; or by more than one of these penalties. (ibid.: 25)

Before this bill could become state law a substitute bill, the Calvin Resolution, passed through the state house and senate and was signed by the governor. The Calvin Resolution read:

> Resolved, by the house of representatives, the senate concurring, That, in the future, the governor be directed not to draw his warrant for the annual appropriation of the sum of $8,000 to the Atlanta University, under the act of March 3, 1874, until such a plan of expenditure as will secure the exclusive use of the same for the education of colored children only, in accordance with the declared and settled policy of this state on the subject of co-education of the races, has been submitted and approved by the commission constituted in said act for the supervision of expenditure of said appropriation. (ibid.: 27)

The Calvin Resolution made clear the posture of White Georgia politicians on the issue of integrated schooling. Funding for Atlanta University was to be withheld until it ended its integrationist mission. However, if another school was established exclusively for the education of Black students before Atlanta University changed its policy, then funds originally earmarked for the disobedient institution would be forwarded to the new school. As if the failed Glenn Bill and successful Calvin Resolution were not enough, days after the latter legislation passed an amended Glenn Bill passed through the state senate. This bill barred schools that embraced integration from receiving state funds and proposed that individuals educated at such institutions be prevented from obtaining a job at "any school in Georgia which was the recipient of public funds" (ibid.: 27). The amended Glenn Bill did not become law. However, the state did enforce the Calvin Resolution. "As neither [Atlanta University nor the state legislature] receded from its position, the relationship between the institution and the state came to an end" (ibid.: 27). Atlanta University, because of its non-discriminatory admissions policy, was permanently denied its annual appropriation of $8,000. Du Bois (1968: 222–223), reflecting on Atlanta University's firm non-discrimination stance, wrote:

> The University from the beginning had taken a strong and unbending attitude toward Negro prejudice and discrimination; white teachers and black students ate together in the same dining room and lived in the same

dormitories. The charter of the institution opened the doors of Atlanta University to any student who applied, of any race or color, and when the state in 1887 objected to the presence of a few white students who were all children of teachers and professors, the institution gave up the small appropriation from the State rather than repudiate its principles. In fact, this appropriation represented not State funds, but the Negroes' share of the sum received from the federal government for education.

Atlanta University, similar to most institutions of higher learning of any era, but especially so for a predominately Black one located in the heart of America's Jim Crow territory, was in dire need of financial resources so that its stated mission and goals could be successfully achieved. Because of the toxic and potentially deadly racial environment in the American South, in general, and Georgia, specifically, the school's mere existence was constantly threatened. In addition to challenges from the state government, the school was often attacked by local media and citizens. According to Elliott Rudwick (1957: 466):

> [N]ot a few Southerners thought of burying the school by means of oppressive taxation. Over the years, local newspapers published a spate of diatribes, and the institution was accused of teaching racial egalitarianism. Northerners on the faculty were looked upon as meddlers seeking to incite Negroes against whites. The General Education Board, which 'stood before [Atlanta] almost as an evil monster,' was unsympathetic with the manner in which the school was governed, since the foundation advocated a rapprochement with the white South and its mores.

An additional loss of revenue occurred in 1892 when the trustees for the John F. Slater Fund withdrew their philanthropic gifts from Atlanta University. This decision was made because, unlike schools such as Tuskegee Institute and Hampton Institute, Atlanta University embraced and promoted a traditional liberal arts curriculum. Because of their refusal to embrace a primarily vocational educational curriculum, monies from the Slater Fund were withdrawn from Atlanta University and reallocated to schools that did embrace vocational and technical education. Instead of bowing to these tremendous pressures and literal threats to the lives of members of its community, Atlanta University steeled itself as it was placed into a position in which its motto, "I Will Find a Way or Make One," was quickly and deeply tested. Despite the school's loss of funding from the state of Georgia and the Slater Fund it still managed to become one of the leading institutions of higher education, Black or White, in the United States and eventually the leading American laboratory of sociological research.

Black Schools and Sociology

Although the majority of Black schools established to educate the newly emancipated freedmen and freedwomen labeled themselves *university* and *college*, the quality of the curriculum and instruction dispensed was not yet equal to that of many established White institutions offering university and college work. For the most part, the curriculum offered at most early Black institutions was equal to that of common and normal schools. Frank Bowles and Frank DeCosta (1971: 29) noted that:

> Literally hundreds of [Black institutions] were founded with 'normal,' 'college,' and 'university' in their titles. Of course, they were largely elementary and secondary schools, but their titles were selected with the aim of indicating the eventual purpose they were to serve.

It must be noted that the teaching of common and normal school, or preparatory, curriculums at universities and colleges was not exclusive to Black institutions. Bowles and DeCosta (ibid.: 31) also noted, for example, that:

> As late as 1895, all the white colleges in Alabama [with the exception of the University of Alabama] reported preparatory enrollments … Even in Massachusetts, Boston College and Tufts College reported preparatory enrollments.

Again, while many early Black institutions were given names that foretold what they were to become, one must be mindful that even the most highly rated of colleges began at levels far from where they would eventually be perched. Augustus F. Beard (1909: 154–155) supports this assessment when he argued that:

> Oxford when it began more than a thousand years ago was not Oxford of to-day. Yale University, which lately celebrated its two hundredth birthday, began when half a dozen ministers of the gospel brought together a few books and said, We give these for the founding of a college. The name is

in the interests and purpose, in the faith of what is to be, and in the hope of final achievement. Let us wait two hundred years and then ask whether or not this [Black institution] was rightly named University.

This passage is important as it places into context the often lengthy and arduous process by which institutions and educational programs develop. Additionally, it should be emphatically pointed out here that, unlike their White counterparts, many Black institutions of higher education were serving simultaneously as elementary, secondary and post-secondary institutions since their pre-emancipation experiences yielded virtually no institutions for the formal and legal education of Blacks. Thus, early Black *universities* and *colleges* provided educational opportunities to Blacks of varying ages and abilities who had heretofore been legally denied, with the tacit support of the United States government, the right to pursue an education. Once granted this human right, Blacks and sympathetic Whites established schools to service the broad range of abilities and needs of the formerly enslaved masses. Essential in the establishment of universities and colleges for Blacks was the expectation, as indicated above, that these institutions would one day be deserving of the titles bestowed upon them. This point was addressed by Edmund Asa Ware, first president of Atlanta University, who often aggressively confronted those who were skeptical that the freedmen and freedwomen would eventually achieve levels of intelligence necessary for the creation of *true* universities and colleges. According to Myron Adams (1930: 24):

Ware had faith in humanity—he believed that all men, regardless of race, were capable of development. This optimism was expressed in the adoption of the name *University* in 1867, for it then signaled nothing save prophecy. Some years later, Ware wrote 'It, [use of University], foretold the capacity of those for whom the school was especially founded, to advance in education, till they should need the advantages of a full university course. It foretold the willingness of the friends of humanity to furnish fulfillment of the first prophecy, provided the second can be accomplished.

President Ware's optimism for Atlanta University's development into a first rate institution of higher learning was affirmed nearly 40 years after its establishment upon the release of a 1910 study on Black colleges and college graduates.

In 1900 W. E. B. Du Bois conducted the first objective and scholarly study on Black colleges and Black college graduates in the United States. Using data from more than 1,000 Black college graduates, Du Bois offered a solid rebuke to the opponents of his talented tenth[5] perspective who believed Blacks should focus more on technical and vocational than liberal arts education. The argument of his opponents was grounded largely on the belief that college educated Blacks would have great difficulty finding employment in early twentieth century America. In his 1900 study Du Bois discovered there was a demand for college trained Blacks and that the graduates of his preferred educational curriculum, the liberal arts, were gainfully employed. An equally important component of the 1900 study was his ranking of the top Black colleges in the nation. Du Bois's ranking was based on each institution's entry requirements, which included the length of preparatory courses, number of years of study devoted to subjects including Latin, Greek, Math and English and the number of weeks of study per year. By this measure, of the more than 30 schools examined, Howard was identified as the only First Rate school because its entrance requirements were nearly equal to the smaller New England Colleges. Second Rate schools, those from one to two years behind the smaller New England colleges, included Fisk, Atlanta, Wilberforce, Leland and Paul Quinn. Third Rate schools, those from two to three years behind the smaller New England colleges included Biddle, Shaw, Virginia N & C and Livingstone.

In 1910 Du Bois revisited the topic of the Black college and Black college graduates. Similar to the 1900 study, he ranked Black colleges using entry requirements. This study, however, utilized admissions requirements as defined by the Carnegie Foundation. By this measure the "standard requirements for admission to college were at least 14 credits, a unit being a course of five periods weekly throughout the academic year of the preparatory school" (Du Bois and Dill 1910: 12). With the Carnegie Foundation for the Advancement of Teaching standards as the measure, the top five ranked Black schools were Howard, Fisk, Atlanta, Wiley and Leland. Each of these 'First Grade Colored Schools' (*sic*) required 14 or

---

5   The talented tenth is the moniker that W. E. B. Du Bois bestowed upon liberal arts trained Black Americans whom he charged with serving in positions of leadership within their communities and the nation. The talented tenth does not refer to a specific and ideal number of leaders. This concept refers to the responsibility that those of "exceptional ability," whether in business, the arts, medicine, etc., have to serve the masses such that the social, economic and physical condition of the race will be improved.

more units of entrance requirements and enrolled more than 20 students in their college units. As measured by this standard, more than ten Black colleges rated equal to or greater than predominately White institutions (PWIs) like the University of North Carolina, University of Virginia, University of Alabama, University of South Carolina and Randolph-Macon College. While Black colleges were beginning to assume legitimate university status among their PWI peers, the discipline of sociology was simultaneously developing as a legitimate academic field in the United States.

In 1918 Luther L. Bernard examined the course offerings of numerous Black and White colleges in an attempt to measure the amount of time devoted to study in sociology as compared to other disciplines. He discovered that history and political science were the most popular courses at PWIs. Bernard (1918: 505) conversely noted, "the institutions for Negroes give, relative to other institutions, little attention either to political science or history. This is not difficult to understand when the political status and the condition of the Negro are taken into consideration." While his 1918 article failed to provide detailed analysis of why instruction in sociology was more popular at Black colleges than PWIs, Bernard revisited the topic in a 1948 article and offered a more focused explanation. Bernard (1948: 14) stated:

> It is apparent that sociology was first accepted by the smaller institutions of the South and by the Negro colleges. The reason for the Negro interest is, I think, sufficiently evident in the fact that a minority group was trying honestly to understand the social situation in which it found itself.

The social situation that Blacks found themselves during the discipline's formative years was Jim Crow segregation, disfranchisement, economic oppression and physical violence imposed by American Whites. Scholars at Black colleges, unlike many of their White peers, viewed sociology as a tool that could be used actively to eliminate or reduce the extreme levels of inequality in the United States.[6]

Additional evidence of the discipline's popularity at Black institutions, especially Atlanta University, can be found in Du Bois's 1910 Atlanta University investigation in which he examined the curriculum of numerous Black post-secondary institutions and noted the amount of

---

6   See Earl Wright II and Thomas C. Calhoun. 2006. "Jim Crow Sociology: Toward An Understanding of Black Sociology via the Atlanta Sociological Laboratory." *Sociological Focus* 39(1): 1–18.

time devoted to the seven major fields of study (i.e., ancient languages, modern languages, natural science, mathematics, English, sociology and history and philosophy). After examining the curriculum of 18 Black post-secondary institutions Du Bois discovered that instruction in the area of sociology and history (which were grouped together) consistently placed third, behind ancient languages and natural sciences, in the percentage of course hours dedicated to each discipline. The schools with the highest percentage of coursework devoted to sociology and history were Atlanta University (19 percent), Claflin (16 percent) and Straight (14 percent). It may well be considered a notable accomplishment for the discipline shortly after its birth, Black colleges, led by Atlanta University, were gainfully engaged in its instruction. However, that Black schools in the American South would use sociology as a tool of empowerment was cause for some to resort to physical, even deadly, measures to ensure that the status quo remained the way that it had been for years—the domination of Whites over Blacks. Owing to the fear of White backlash from the teaching of sociology in such a manner that risked making some Blacks 'uppity', Atlanta University, although using academic texts, *taught around sociology*.

Teaching around Sociology

Between 1889 and 1894 John Howard Hincks served as Professor of Social Science and History as well as Dean of Faculty at Atlanta University. He was brought to the institution by his Yale classmate, Atlanta University President Horace Bumstead, because both shared a desire to assist in the improvement of the condition of Blacks in America and, thereby, improvement of the nation as a whole. No institution in the nation was better situated to accomplish this goal than Atlanta University since this idea was promoted within its community by deed and word. Moreover, it was understood, even if tacitly, that the new discipline of sociology would be a useful and important tool in the effort to improve the condition of Blacks in the United States. Russell W. Irvine (2001: 259) noted:

> The faculty of Atlanta University were principally interested in training leaders for work among blacks in the south. Knowledge of how the world is organized, what principles drove it, what motivated people within it, and how human relationships are ordered was essential to the work of leading a newly freed population. Graduates of Atlanta University were

conceived of as agents of change and directors of the affairs of the black community. It was imperative, if for no other reason, that they knew how the world they were charged to lead worked. (my emphasis)

This was an un(der)stated objective since school officials were acutely aware of the dangers this type of posture posed for themselves and their students. That the American South was the central location of the majority of lynchings of Blacks was not lost on the leaders of the all-Black institution. It is for this reason that the emancipatory discipline, if such an area of study actually exists, was circuitously infused into the school's curriculum. "Perceptively and wisely the leadership of Atlanta University understood that the force of ideas can wreak havoc as surely as weapons of personal injury. For that reason, rather than teach sociology per se, they chose to teach around it" (ibid.: 251). While it is plausible that early sociology texts like Franklin Giddings's *Elements of Sociology* and *Principles of Sociology*, Albion Small's *Introduction to a Science of Society*, William Sumner's *Study of Sociology* and Lester Ward's *Dynamic Sociology* could have been adopted, the books selected for student consumption were James Fairchild's *Moral Philosophy; or the Science of Obligation*, Francois P. Guizot's *History of Civilization in Europe* and Francis Wayland's *Political Economy*. The latter two books were the principal social science texts and the former was used to teach history. The social science texts were selected for a number of reasons. First, both authors were college presidents, highly regarded scholars and not terribly infected with the plague of race hatred. Thus, Atlanta University students were secretly taught the liberating potential of sociology via books that did not wholly extract them from the community of humanity. Additionally, Irvine (ibid.: 254) writes that the textbook selectors also "regarded the substance of their work not only as evidence of the best scholarship available at the time, but it was also thought that both men were sympathetic to the plight of blacks in America. The selection of their texts was a form of honor to their loyalty in the antislavery era."

Despite the commitment of White Atlanta University faculty to the uplift of Blacks in America, there was agreement that the advancement of the race would have to be led primarily by Blacks themselves. "Hincks could offer friendship and sympathy," according to Irvine (ibid.: 262), "but [he] could not have called or led them to battle" ... "Hincks could intellectually carry students at Atlanta University so far" (ibid.: 261). It is ironic that Hincks, the person principally responsible for establishing the foundation upon which the tremendous sociological accomplishments that would soon arise, died in 1894. One year before the school approved a request to establish a program of scientific research on Blacks in America and three years before the arrival of Du Bois to its campus, Hincks's untimely death due to complications from typhoid prevented him from witnessing, arguably, the greatest program of sociological inquiry of the twentieth century in the United States.

Chapter 2
"We Study the Problems That Others Talk About"

John H. Hincks laid the foundation for the establishment of a department of sociology during his brief tenure at Atlanta University from 1889 to 1894. Within two years of his death sociology was no longer taught in a clandestine manner. Instead, it was a prominent component of the Department of Political & Social Science and History. The *Catalogue of the Officers and Students of Atlanta University* indicates that, while sociology was not yet a formalized department, its instruction was central to the unit. According to the catalogue:

> It is intended to develop this department more fully, especially along the line of Sociology. Interest has been awakened throughout the country in the annual conferences held at Atlanta University in May—the first in 1896—concerning problems in city life among the colored population. The library will soon be rich in books pertaining to Sociology. (Atlanta University 1897: 31)

By 1898 Atlanta University had established a department that included sociology in the title. The mission of the Department of Sociology and History was clear.

> It is intended to develop this department not only for the sake of mental discipline, but also in order to familiarize our students with the history of nations and with the great economic and social problems of the world. It is hoped that thus they may be able to apply broad and careful knowledge to the solving of the many intricate questions affecting their own people. The department aims therefore at training in good intelligent leadership; at a thorough comprehension of the chief problems of wealth, work and wages; and at a fair knowledge of the objects and methods of social reform. (Atlanta University 1899: 13)

Textbooks used by sociology students included *Civil Government* by Fiske, *The State* by Wilson, *Economics* by Hadley and *Statistics and Sociology* by Mayo-Smith. In addition to the instruction of undergraduates, graduate instruction was offered within the department and research experience was garnered by both via the sociological research program established three years earlier.

In 1895 Atlanta University President Horace Bumstead presented a proposal to the school's board of trustees requesting the establishment of a yearly program of research into the social, economic and physical condition of Blacks making the transition from slavery to freedom and rural to city life. The idea for this research program came from Atlanta University graduates who often communicated with their former teachers and administrators about the changing societal landscape and the need for scientific study of the social problems in their communities. That school administrators would approve the proposal on July 1, 1895 was a certainty since:

> Atlanta University always [drew] its students exclusively from the cities and large towns, and a great portion of its graduates [were] holding positions at these centers of influence. From these workers information [came] to the faculty and trustees of the University from time to time that led them to believe there exist[ed] a great need for a systematic and thorough investigation into the conditions of living among the Negro population of cities. (Atlanta University 1896: 5)

After the proposal was approved it was decided that the first conference would take place later that year during the Atlanta Exposition. Ironically, the 1895 Atlanta Exposition is where Booker T. Washington delivered his (in)famous 'Atlanta Compromise' speech where he acquiesced to the segregationist policies of American Jim Crow legislation in exchange for increased economic opportunities for Blacks. While no evidence exists to suggest that the timing of the Atlanta Exposition or Washington's speech caused its delay, "after further consideration, it was deemed wise to change the time [of the inaugural conference of the Atlanta University Study of the Negro Problem] to the Commencement in May, 1896" (ibid.: 5).

The 1896 and 1897 investigations were led by George G. Bradford, an Atlanta University trustee who was selected because of his 'passing interest in Negro issues,' and designed to address topics not explored at conferences held at other Black institutions. The Atlanta University Study of the Negro Problem, with its motto "We Study the Problems that Others Talk About," was conceptualized to embody the urban manifestation of the existing Hampton Institute and Tuskegee Institute conferences. According to Du Bois (1968: 212-213):

> This program was grafted on an attempt by George Bradford of Boston, one of the [school's] trustees, to open for Atlanta University a field of usefulness for city Negroes comparable to what Hampton and Tuskegee were doing for rural districts in agriculture and industry. At the Hampton and Tuskegee Conferences, there came together annually and in increasing numbers,

workers, experts, and observers to encourage by speeches and interchange of experience the Negro farmers and laborers of adjoining areas. Visitors, white and colored, from North and South, joined to advise and learn. Mr. Bradford's idea was to establish at Atlanta a similar conference, devoted especially to problems of city Negroes.

Under Bradford's leadership two monographs were published and two conferences organized. Despite Bradford's competent service as director of the inaugural studies and conferences, school officials wanted the leader of their research program to have academic training in the social sciences and for that person to provide leadership and vision for a program of research on Blacks that would, ideally, lead to improvements in their social, economic and physical condition in the United States. Moreover, they wanted someone who could implement a scholarly and rigorous research agenda on the pressing issues of the day. It did not take long for Atlanta University officials to secure the services of the most skilled social scientist of the era, W. E. B. Du Bois.

After completing *The Philadelphia Negro*, a groundbreaking book that stands as the first urban sociological study conducted in the United States, Du Bois desired to establish a long term program of research on Blacks to offset the biased and unscientific *car window sociology*[1] studies littering the existing sociological and social science literature at the turn of the twentieth century. Reflecting on this idea in a recorded 1961 interview, Du Bois (1961: 3) asserted, "what we needed was an academic study of the American Negro. I wanted the universities of Pennsylvania and Harvard and Yale and so forth to go into a sort of partnership by which this kind of study could be forwarded." To his dismay, the proposed consortium of Ivy League schools was not receptive to his idea of establishing a research program centered on American Blacks. "But Atlanta University," Du Bois (ibid.: 3) said, "asked me to come down there and teach and take charge of some such study. So that in 1897 I went to Atlanta University."

President Bumstead, in a 1918 letter reflecting on his decision to hire Du Bois, wrote about "the keen satisfaction I take in having been the one chiefly responsible, perhaps, for bringing Doctor Du Bois to Atlanta University" (Bumstead [1918] 1981: 1). Describing the desired characteristics for the leader of the research program, he stated that "We wanted a professor of sociology with special reference to investigating conditions concerning the

---

1 In *Souls of Black Folk*, Du Bois argued that many White sociologists and social scientists often conducted scientific investigations into the social lives of Blacks in America by causally observing their interactions from afar for brief moments then using that data to develop grand theories on the entire race. Du Bois called this practice "car window sociology".

Negro; I said that Doctor Du Bois was the one man, white or black, far and away best fitted for the position" (ibid.: 1). Despite President Bumstead's confidence in Du Bois's talents, some Atlanta University officials believed this position should be reserved for an alumnus of Atlanta University. President Bumstead recounted certain school officials asking, "If you are going to give the position to a Negro why not [give it] to a graduate of Atlanta [University] rather than Fisk [University]?" (ibid.: 2) President Bumstead's reply was simply, "Because we want the best man, regardless of where he was graduated" (ibid.: 2). Continuing the letter wherein he discussed Du Bois's qualifications for the position, President Bumstead wrote:

> [I] knew of [Du Bois's] long preparation at Fisk, Harvard, and in Germany, and I had read the unstinted praise which the New York Nation had given to his first publication, "The Suppression of the Slave Trade," and I knew of the confidence which Provost Harrison of the University of Pennsylvania had in him when he engaged him to a year or more in making a scientific study of the Philadelphia Negro. (ibid.: 2)

In his concluding paragraph President Bumstead acknowledged the obstacles to Du Bois's hiring and the significance of his career long accomplishments at the institution.

> In spite of objections and misgivings, Doctor Du Bois came to Atlanta University, and we held him there for thirteen years notwithstanding several offers to go elsewhere and get double the salary that we could afford to pay him. His work became a memorable part of the Institution. (ibid.: 2)

When Du Bois arrived in Atlanta he quickly discovered that the existing research program did not meet his rigorous scholarly standards. In a highly critical review of Bradford's 1896 and 1897 efforts, Du Bois stated that "as a scientific accomplishment the first conference was not important" (Du Bois [1940] 1981: 797) and of low scientific value because "[the investigations] followed the Hampton and Tuskegee model of being primarily meetings of inspiration, directed toward specific efforts at social reform and aimed at propaganda for social uplift in certain preconceived lines" (Du Bois 1968: 214). What Du Bois envisioned was the establishment of a research program that employed the most advanced practices in research methods and scholarly inquiry while producing objective scientific studies on the social, economic and physical condition of Blacks in America. In some cases, Du Bois and members of the Atlanta Sociological Laboratory had to create research methods and investigative practices, some of which still today are institutionalized in social science disciplines, since the necessary tools to accomplish their research objectives had not yet been established. However, a primary objective upon arriving in Atlanta was the implementation of his brand of research while distancing himself from that established by Bradford.

Upon assuming leadership of the investigation Du Bois "did not pause to consider how far [his] developed plans agreed or disagreed with the ideas of the already launched project" (ibid.: 214). Du Bois ([1940] 1981: 62), some years later, asserted that:

> Without any thought or consultation I rather peremptorily changed the plans of the first two Atlanta Conferences. They had been conceived as conferences limited to city problems, contrasting with the increasing popular conferences on rural problems held at Tuskegee. But I was not thinking of mere conferences. I was thinking of a comprehensive plan for studying a human group.

Moreover, Du Bois (1968: 214) had definite plans on how his research laboratory should be run.

> This program at Atlanta, I sought to swing as on a pivot to one of scientific investigation into social conditions, primarily for scientific ends. I put no special effort on special reform effort, but increasing and widening emphasis on the collection of a basic body of fact concerning the social condition of American Negroes, endeavoring to reduce that condition to exact measurement whenever or wherever occasion permitted.

Du Bois's ultimate objective was to upgrade the investigations from purely descriptive analyses of human behavior and the collection of census type data to one grounded in rigorous scientific truths and systematic inquiry.

A major adjustment that he made in the effort to make the investigation more scientific was to focus on one specific aspect of Black life instead of a hodgepodge of issues as Bradford's plan suggested. According to Du Bois ([1940] 1981: 3):

> Instead of trying to study the whole mass of social conditions and discuss the whole Negro problem, I deliberately put an 's' upon 'problem' and emphasized the study of negro problems and then took up one problem or one phase of a social problem affecting Negroes for a year's intensive study.

Du Bois ([1904] 1978: 58) continued:

> The method employed is to divide the various aspects of [the condition of African Americans] into ten great subjects. To treat one of these subjects each year as carefully and exhaustively as means will allow until the cycle is

completed. To begin then again on the same cycle for a second ten years. So that in the course of a century, if the work is well done we shall have a continuous record on the condition and development of a group of 10 to 20 million of men—a body of sociological material unsurpassed in human annals.

Repeatedly, Du Bois wanted to secure a 100-year body of sociological data on Blacks in America. These data would be used to construct a theory on the social and economic development of Blacks in the United States. Reflecting on this idea in his autobiography, Du Bois (1968: 217) wrote:

I laid down an ambitious program for a hundred years of study. I proposed to take up annually in each decade the main aspects of the group life of Negroes with as thorough study and measurement as possible, and repeat the same program in the succeeding decade with additions, changes and better methods.

While Du Bois was not able to amass 100 years of data, he did successfully lead the first program of objective and scientific inquiry into the social, economic and physical condition of Blacks in the United States. What follows is a review of the 20 volumes of the Atlanta University studies, 16 led entirely or in part by Du Bois, conducted between 1896 and 1917.

The Atlanta University Study of the Negro Problems, 1896–1917

Between 1896 and 1917 the Atlanta Sociological Laboratory published 20 volumes of the Atlanta University Study of the Negro Problems. W. E. B. Du Bois spearheaded the preparation of 16 monographs (four in collaboration with Augustus Granville Dill), Atlanta University is credited with preparing two monographs and Thomas I. Brown and J. A. Bigham each prepared one monograph. The following section includes a detailed overview of each publication. However, before a review of the publications is presented I want to proactively address why such a mundane task, at least in the eyes of some, is necessary. This task is undertaken for three reasons. First, the existing literature on W. E. B. Du Bois currently includes no detailed articulation of what he and the members of the Atlanta Sociological Laboratory actually accomplished and how. Despite the fact that the largest organization of professional sociologists in the United States, the American Sociological Association, recently renamed its highest honor in his name, when Du Bois's career is discussed his years as a practicing sociologist at Atlanta University are either totally ignored or awarded only cursory attention. The primary exceptions to this assertion, this author's past works notwithstanding, are Nagueyalti Warren who, even in her book on Du Bois's status as the Godfather of Black Studies, offers only an abbreviated summary of the studies and not a detailed presentation of the kind that follows here, and Shaun L. Gabbidon, who writes about Du Bois's contributions to criminal justice. It is incredible that, arguably, Du Bois's most significant contributions to the discipline have not been as thoroughly mined and exhaustively analyzed as those of his highly regarded peers. Second, the detailed presentation of this school's sociological research accomplishments is necessary as it can be easily accessed for purposes of comparison with the scholarly products of its peers; namely, the vaunted and highly regarded Chicago School of Sociology—the name bestowed on scholars engaged in sociological inquiry at the University of Chicago, circa 1915–1940. Last, the presentation of this information is necessary because it forms the foundation for the arguments made in Chapter 3 concerning the school's significant contributions to sociology. Accordingly, what follows is a detailed presentation, when applicable, of the methods of data collection, findings and resolutions (theories) of the Atlanta University Studies of the Negro Problems, 1896–1917.

Atlanta University Publication #1, 1896
"Mortality among Negroes in Cities"
Editor Unknown

The first Atlanta University investigation, conference, and publication focused on "Mortality among Negroes in Cities." This subject was selected by George G. Bradford, lead researcher of the 1896 and 1897 studies, because "In taking up the study of city problems, we feel that we cannot do better than begin by an inquiry into the physical and moral condition of the people. It is a line of inquiry which has not been previously pursued on any systematic or extensive scale. [Additionally], of the [study of the] physical condition of the Negro under the trying conditions of city life, we have little information" (Atlanta University 1896: 8).

Bradford's data were not obtained through a rigorous methodology. Instead, the findings of this investigation were based on blanks, census data and encyclopedic facts. Atlanta University officials readily acknowledged the limitations of their first investigation, but remained steadfast in their belief that scientific findings grounded in a rigorous methodology was their desired goal and would soon become the normative expectation for subsequent studies. President Bumstead, speaking to attendees at the first conference, said:

> It was not expected that much in the line of scientific reports based upon
> accurate data could be presented at this first conference, but it was believed
> that much information could be gathered from the ordinary experiences and
> observations of graduates and others, and that the subject could be considered
> in such a manner as to arouse interest and enthusiasm, and so pave the way for
> collecting and digesting extensive and accurate data. Such it is believed, has
> been the result of the conference held. (ibid.: 5)

Bradford and Bumstead convened the inaugural conference knowing the data
from this investigation centered more on observational data than systematic
inquiry and scientific facts garnered by researchers. Despite this publicly
acknowledged limitation, Bumstead commended the researchers for their
efforts and declared his commitment to securing the services of a trained
social scientist to take leadership of the research program such that more
extensive and accurate data could be garnered utilizing the most advanced
scientific methods of the era.

The methods of data collection used in the first investigation were blanks
and census data. While they were called blanks at the turn of the century,
this research instrument is known today as a questionnaire. "Uniform sets
of blanks [were] prepared and put into the hands of graduates of [Atlanta]
University and of educated colored men and women located in different cities"
(ibid.: 9). It is not exactly known to whom blanks were distributed for this
investigation. However, conference records indicate that data were received
from citizen researchers in Atlanta, GA, Savannah, GA, and Washington, D.C.

Three sets of blanks were collected from each household participating in
this investigation. "Blanks No. 1 and 2 [served] the purpose of a permanent
record by which to measure the progress of each city community from year
to year [and] Blank No. 3, called the Family Budget blank, provides for a
more intimate inquiry into the conditions of life existing in a particular
community" (ibid.: 9). The data collected from Blank No. 1 centered on the
general condition of home life, size of the home, sanitary conditions inside the
home and amount of sickness in the home. Data collected from Blank No. 2
focused on the economic condition of the family, occupations of working
family members and amount of income earned by each family member. Data
collected from Blank No. 3 aimed at ascertaining the expenditures of each
family for food, rent, alcohol and extravagance. Atlanta University researchers
analyzed the three sets of blanks and proposed that the expenditures
investigated in Blank No. 3 caused the conditions faced in Blanks No. 1 and 2.
Although they hypothesized that the conditions experienced in Blanks No. 1
and 2 resulted from the spending practices recorded in Blank No. 3, Atlanta
University researchers ardently asserted that they were not attempting to
develop a grand theory on the condition of Blacks in cities based upon these

limited data. In fact, George G. Bradford stated, "We are not attempting to prove or disprove any theory, but we are trying to get at the most unfavorable conditions affecting our communities, in order that we may improve those conditions" (ibid.: 10).

1890 United States Census data were used to examine the rates of "mortality for the white and colored population of five of our largest cities" (ibid.: 8). The cities included in this investigation were Baltimore, MD, Louisville, KY, New Orleans, LA, St. Louis, MO, and Washington, D.C. These data were used comparatively with blanks to discern the major causes of death among Blacks in cities and provided the foundation for the major findings presented in the resolutions of this conference.

The first resolution of the 1896 Atlanta University conference asserted that, according to United States Census Bureau data, there was an increase in the death rate of Blacks between the years 1880 and 1890. "Comparing [1880 figures] with those for 1890, we see that the latter year shows a greater actual and relative death-rate from those diseases. The conclusion to be drawn from this comparison would be that consumption and pneumonia were on the increase among colored people for the decade 1880–1890" (ibid.: 15). Bradford and conference officials suggested that the prevalence of these diseases was the result of ignorance, poverty, negligence and intemperance by Blacks. The second resolution of the 1896 conference proposed that "the investigations thus far made show the necessity for continuing the search for exact data on a large scale, with a view to ascertaining more definitely the causes and seeking out and applying remedies for existing conditions" (ibid.: 24). The third resolution was a recommendation to the corresponding secretary and executive committee that the annual conference be continued the following year and that graduates of Atlanta University and all others interested in studying the condition of Blacks in cities be invited to participate in future investigations.

While the inaugural 1896 conference did not produce findings that dramatically impacted the literature on the social, economic or physical condition of Blacks in the United States, as the major discovery was that the death rate for Blacks was higher than that of Whites, the importance of this investigation is that it comprised the first attempt at objectively and scientifically studying the condition of Blacks in America.

Atlanta University Publication #2, 1897
"Social and Physical Condition of Negroes in Cities"
Editor Unknown

The subject of the 1897 investigation, conference and publication, "Social and Physical Condition of Negroes in Cities," was an extension of the first conference. Specifically, "[this] investigation was begun [in 1895] by an inquiry on the part of three graduates of Atlanta University into the causes of the excessive mortality among Negroes" (Atlanta University 1897: 3). Atlanta University officials believed "the facts brought out at [the 1896] conference were so significant that the investigation [should be] continued for another year along similar lines, but on a more extensive scale" (ibid.: 3). Unlike the first monograph, the data collection techniques were not clearly identified. It can be discerned, however, that data were obtained through the use of blanks, reports from Boards of Health and an investigation into the social and physical conditions obtained in various southern cities.

No specific information concerning the content of the blanks used in this inquiry was found. It is proposed, however, that since this was a continuation of the previous year's study the information obtained via blanks for the 1896 study were used here also. The only information concerning blanks for the 1897 study was that data were collected from 1,137 families.

L. M. Hershaw was charged with the "laborious work of analyzing the reports of the boards of health for the past fifteen years" (ibid.: 5). The cities where health data reports were collected included Atlanta, GA, Baltimore, MD, Charleston, SC, Memphis, TN, and Richmond, VA. These data were utilized to ascertain the causes and rates of mortality of Blacks in the cities identified. Professor Eugene Harris of Fisk University served as the lead researcher of an investigation focused on the social and physical condition of southern Blacks. Once again, the specific method(s) of research were not cited. However, as best can be deciphered, Harris utilized data collected from over 18 cities by graduates of various Black institutions and citizen researchers. Additionally, data from the May Bulletin of the Department of Labor were utilized to identify the specific occupations held by Blacks during this period.

As introduced earlier, Atlanta University used as data collectors faculty, undergraduate and graduate students from that institution, other predominately Black schools and regular citizens interested in investigating and improving the social, economic and physical condition of Blacks in America. Accordingly, conference officials recognized graduates of Atlanta University (50), Fisk University (30), Berea College (15), Lincoln University, Spelman College, Howard University, and Meharry Medical College for their assistance in collecting data for the 1896 and 1897 studies. While not practiced to any great extent today, the measure of employing the talents of non-trained social scientists as data collectors was a practical necessity that the Atlanta Sociological Laboratory embraced and worked to perfect. Butler R. Wilson, member of a research team that collected data on 100 families that migrated from North Carolina to Cambridge, Massachusetts, explained the process of selecting researchers for this investigation and the benefit of utilizing not only

Atlanta University graduates and students, but Black "citizen researchers" in general.

> The results to be gained [for this investigation] depend entirely upon the intelligence and fitness of the investigators, who were selected with great care from the ranks of well-known colored educators, ministers, physicians, lawyers and businessmen, living among the people covered by the investigation. All the data were gathered by this body of trained colored leaders, and are believed to be, perhaps, more than usually accurate because of the investigators' knowledge of the character, habits and prejudices of the people, and because of the fact that they were not hindered by the suspicions which confront the white investigator, and which seriously affect the accuracy of the answers to his questions. (ibid.: 5)

What must not be missed here is the racial climate that existed in America during this time. Slavery had only been formally ruled unconstitutional for 31 years. Despite this fact, shadow slavery programs called sharecropping and the convict leasing system coalesced with American Jim Crow legislation to create slave-like living conditions for Blacks in the South. When White researchers ventured into the rural South seeking data from members of Black communities, even if they were well-intentioned, they often found it very difficult to gain accurate information from Black populations. Blacks were hesitant to talk, in part, because they were leery of how that information could possibly be used against them; especially in a region of the country where lynching, murder and attacks on Blacks was a nearly everyday occurrence for reasons as slight as being *disrespectful* to Whites by looking them directly into their eyes or not stepping off the sidewalk upon their approach. This data collection problem necessitated the school's employment of the insider researcher. While this technique is widely embraced and employed now, it must be noted that it was institutionalized at Atlanta University long before it became common practice in the social sciences. Bradford and Atlanta University officials believed the use of citizen researchers, or insider researchers, provided them the ability to obtain data that White researchers could not procure. Additionally, they believed that an all-Black research team would be better situated to analyze and understand social behaviors and/or habits that could, possibly, be misinterpreted by non-Black researchers given the theories of scientific racism that were held at that time (and are discussed in Chapter 3). Through the use of citizen researchers and the other data collection techniques identified herein, the executive committee of the Atlanta University conference offered five resolutions and four recommendations.

The first resolution asserted that the high death rate among Blacks was not mainly due to their environment. This conclusion was based on health board reports and census data which revealed that "the rate [of death for African Americans] has decreased [over the past fifteen years] … in the face of hard, exacting and oppressive social and economic conditions" (ibid.: 18). Researchers asserted that if the environment were the main contributor to the death rate of Blacks, the number of deaths would have increased over the past 15 years instead of decreasing. In fact, Atlanta University officials argued that "The history of weak and inferior races shows that they begin to decrease in number after one generation's contact with Anglo-Saxon civilization … We do not witness this decay and decrease in numbers in the colored race any where in the Western Hemisphere" (ibid.: 18). Thus, Atlanta University officials were left pondering, "When all of the facts in the colored man's case are taken into consideration, the wonder is, not that the death-rate is as high as it is, but that it is not even higher" (ibid.: 18).

The second resolution stated that the high rate of death among Blacks in cities was due mostly to their "ignorance or disregard of the laws of health and morality" (ibid.: 33). Eugene Harris noted that:

> In public conveniences the Negro must take separate apartments; but the air in them is just as invigorating, the water is just as healthful and pure, and the food is just as nourishing as in the apartments for the whites. Regular bathing will throw off dead matter through the skin, and control of the appetites will contribute largely to health in Negro quarters as well as anywhere else. (ibid.: 20)

Relatedly, the 1896 Atlanta University study supported this resolution where is was indicated that some Black workers "drive or walk all day in the rain or snow, come home and go to bed with his wet cloths (*sic*) on, with the belief firmly fixed in his mind that unless he lets these cloths dry on him he will contract a cold, and no argument we might use will convince him otherwise" (Atlanta University 1896: 16). Additionally, Harris reported on the disregard of morality that, supposedly, contributed to the high rates of death for Blacks:

> It is true that much of the moral laxity which exists among us today arose out of slavery. It is due to a system which whipped women, which dispensed with the institution of marriage, which separated wives from husbands and assigned them to other men, which ruthlessly destroyed female virtue, and which made helpless women the abject tools of their masters. This is the correct explanation of our social status today, but to explain it is not to excuse it. (Atlanta University 1897: 27)

While Atlanta University officials did an excellent job in identifying the social problems experienced by Blacks in urban areas, they can be perceived to adhere to a *blame the victim* perspective while not fully exploring additional factors that may or may not have led to the situation as it existed. A structural examination of the factors leading to the high rates of Black mortality by Atlanta University researchers could possibly have led to additional conclusions.

The third resolution stated that the high death rate and increase in immorality among Blacks was due mostly to the neglect of the home by both parents; especially mothers who were compelled, because of the need to supplement the family income, to work outside of the home. This proposition was the continuation of an argument made at the 1896 conference where it was proposed:

> It may be that the work of the mother of the family requires that she be away from home all day. Leaving at six a.m., without giving any care to the house or children, she returns at eight o'clock at night. The children are asleep, in the street, or at some neighbor's, where they have been all day. The tired mother, after a few words, goes to bed. She awakes next day only to carry out the same program. (Atlanta University 1896: 19)

This passage also could be interpreted as a continuation of the *blame the victim* posture since the implication is that increased immorality and death were caused, primarily, by working Black mothers who did not provide guidance, protection or nurturance for their children. The unprotected children, by this theory, were then left exposed as possible victims of city life. Possibly, emphasis on structural factors (e.g., the need of Black women to work outside the home to, possibly, supplement the income of their spouse, the absence of Black fathers, etc.) that necessitated Black women to work outside of the home, especially during an era when the majority of White women were homemakers, would have offered a more holistic and salient understanding of the social problems identified.

The fourth resolution asserted that the inability of Black men to adequately support their family harmed the race socially, physically and economically. This proposition was not supported by empirical data. Similar to the proposal that the high rates of death among Blacks was not due to their environment, Eugene Harris asserted, "There is no black law upon our statute books regulating [the] private habits [of Black males], or imposing upon him unsanitary surroundings, or restricting him to deleterious occupations, or forcing him to immoderate indulgences" (Atlanta University 1897: 20). Harris and the executive committee suggested that individual, not societal, factors contributed to the social, physical and economic well-being of Black men. Once again, the individual responsibility critique was made without fully taking into consideration the social structures that, often, inhibited Black men from fulfilling the traditional gender roles expected of them.

The fifth resolution proposed that if Blacks relinquished their dependence on charity and charitable organizations and took control of their own destiny, they could become an independent people. This resolution was not rooted in data but grounded in Atlanta University President Asa E. Ware's proposal that this series of investigations be carried out mostly, but not exclusively, by Blacks. President Ware argued that Blacks must lift themselves up by their bootstraps in order to prove their value to White America. Whites could assist in assaults on notions of the physical and biological inferiority of Blacks, but only Blacks themselves could lead this fight. In addition to the resolutions offered above, the executive committee made recommendations addressing the matter of how the Black community could solve the problems identified above.

The first recommendation made by the committee was to continue this line of inquiry at the next year's meeting and the topic of that meeting would center on the family life of Blacks. The second recommendation asserted that parents' associations and mothers' meetings should be organized for the annual conference to provide better guidance for young Black boys and girls. According to Atlanta University officials, parents' associations and mothers' meetings could, possibly, offset the deleterious effects of having a large number of working mothers. Relatedly, the third recommendation called for the establishment of nurseries to provide care for the infants of parents who must work. The fourth and fifth recommendations requested that organizations and individuals visit the poor and that regular meetings be held to discuss the distinct experiences of each visitor.

The 1897 conference, similar to the first, was of limited scientific value and could be interpreted as promoting a *blame the victim* agenda without sufficient analysis of structural factors affecting the condition of Blacks in America. Nevertheless, this investigation, conference and publication were important because Atlanta University officials were continuing to amass data on a subject that had heretofore received little objective scientific treatment.

Atlanta University Publication #3, 1898
"Some Efforts of American Negroes for Their Own Social Betterment"
Edited by W. E. B. Du Bois

The 1898 Atlanta University effort, "Some Efforts of American Negroes for Their Own Social Betterment," was the first investigation lead by W. E. B. Du Bois. Du Bois, who took charge of the Atlanta University studies in January 1897, quickly altered the previously low scientific format of the research program into his brand of scientific inquiry that included, when possible, nationally representative samples, triangulation of data collection, data comparison and theoretical analysis. Du Bois's quest for scientific accuracy began with an inquiry into social programs established by Black organizations that were designed to improve the condition of the race.

Du Bois originally wanted to collect a nationally representative sample of data. Unfortunately, and what proved to be a recurring theme throughout his tenure at Atlanta University, "funds were not available for such an inquiry" (Du Bois 1898: 4). Instead of having a nationally representative sample, Du Bois chose "nine Southern cities of varying size and ... selected in them such organizations of Negroes as were engaged in benevolent and reformatory work" (ibid.: 4). The cities included in this investigation were Atlanta, GA, Augusta, GA, Bowling Green, KY, Clarksville, TN, Fort Smith, AR, Galveston, TX, Mobile, AL, Petersburg, VA and Washington, D.C.

Du Bois relied upon each organization contacted to return a set of questionnaires that were mailed to them. The exact information requested on the questionnaires concerned the current enrollment of the organization, value of real estate, amount of indebtedness, cash on hand, total income, existence of literary societies, objects of expenditures and activities promoting social uplift. Du Bois asserted that this investigation was not an attempt to "catalogue all charitable and reformatory efforts but rather to illustrate the character of work being done by typical examples" (ibid.: 4). Because of their inability to obtain a nationally representative sample of Black organizations, Atlanta University researchers were not able to make any claims regarding generalizability. However, they believed their data to be reliable and valid enough to form a solid foundation for the resolutions.

The first resolution challenged churches to minimize expenses related to regular church operations and, instead, reallocate those funds to the establishment of much needed shelters for the elderly and orphans. For example, Nineteenth St. Baptist Church in Washington, D.C. reported a total 1895 income of $5,714.09. After operating expenses were subtracted the church was left with only $437. Conference officials suggested that expenditures such as the $2,840 spent on building improvements were unnecessary and detracted from the uplifting mission of the church. Additionally, data indicated a paucity of retirement homes and orphanages serving the needs of Blacks in the areas surveyed. Instead of relying upon charitable organizations, conference officials charged Black organizations, specifically churches, with the obligation of supporting and establishing these much needed institutions. Heretofore, the options available for Blacks in need of these services were limited because of racism and segregation.

The second resolution advised secret societies to not spend as much money on 'pomp and circumstance' but, instead, use their money more constructively. Atlanta University data indicated that:

> The secret societies represent much extravagance and waste in expenditure, an outlay for regalia and tinsel, which too often lack the excuse of being beautiful, and to some extent they divert the savings of Negroes from more useful channels. (ibid.: 17)

According to the executive committee more benefits could be derived from spending money on community needs such as retirement homes and orphanages than on wasteful displays of organizational profusion.

The third resolution was a warning to Blacks across the nation. They were advised to be aware of unscrupulous and corrupt insurance companies. Specifically, Blacks were warned that there were "white societies organized to defraud and exploit Negroes" (ibid.: 19). The executive committee proposed that Blacks were likely targets for exploitation by White businesses since "the Freedman [was] noted for his effort to ward off accidents and a pauper's grave by insurance against sickness and death" (ibid.: 19). Many dishonest White businesspersons viewed this as an opportunity to exploit the freedmen and freedwomen who were only recently becoming formally educated and financially literate.

The fourth resolution commended a few beneficial societies for serving the Black community well through systematic works centered on uplifting the community, both socially and economically. Data from beneficial societies in Galveston, TX, Augusta, GA and Atlanta, GA, for example, provided evidence of philanthropic programs and social activities directed at improving the social, economic and physical condition of Blacks in America. Atlanta University officials specifically noted the amount of sick and death benefits offered by some beneficial associations as primary reasons for their acknowledgment.

The fifth resolution charged Blacks with the task of engaging in better financial practices when it came to expenses related to funerals. Data revealed that an extraordinary amount of money was often expended on funerals. Atlanta University researchers believed the monies spent on funerals could be utilized more fruitfully. The executive committee believed "the system of death benefits often encourages this [overspending]. [Thus,] societies giving death benefits, churches, and thoughtful persons in general, should frown upon these excesses as wasteful, unbecoming and unchristian" (ibid.: 47). Instead, they believed it more prudent for Blacks to use some of the money spent on funerals to improve the condition of their immediate family and/or community.

The sixth resolution requested more cooperation between Black businesses. It was believed that cooperative efforts between Blacks would reduce their economic dependence on Whites. Independence on the part of Black entrepreneurs would, hopefully, enable the race to build a solid economic foundation whereby they could better serve the needs of Black communities. The 1898 Atlanta University study recorded a successful cooperative businesses endeavor in Hampton, Virginia.

> These are all incorporated companies, officered and controlled by colored men. They have been organized and operated as an outgrowth directly of the demands of the people rather than as a speculative investment in the different forms of business in rivalry of those already in existence; and to this extent they have all been successful. (ibid.: 25)

Researchers cited comparable levels of success for cooperative business enterprises in cities such as Birmingham, AL, Little Rock, AR, Jacksonville, FL, Richmond, VA and Galveston, TX.

The seventh resolution promoted the establishment of social service providers for Black communities. Specifically, the executive committee stressed the need for hospitals and juvenile reformatories to serve the needs of Blacks. Dr. R. H. Lewis, Secretary of the North Carolina Board of Health and contributor to the 1897 study, expressed the need for these services.

> If there is one thing more than another that the colored people need, it is hospital privileges, practically within their reach, both as to distance and cost. It has been a matter of surprise with me that some of the people of the North, who have been so generous in their benefactions to educational instructions for them, have not realized this fact and devoted some of it to the relief of sickness and suffering. (ibid.: 33)

Atlanta University officials also called for the establishment of juvenile reformatories. It was theorized that such institutions could possibly prevent wayward youth from becoming permanent clogs within the criminal justice system. Data from the state of Virginia was used to support their argument. It was found that the state was:

> Unconsciously ... graduating under common and statute laws annually thousands of youthful criminals. There is no middle ground, there is no house of refuge, correction or reformatory for the black boy or girl—who from defective, and from no training, has taken the first step downward, and as a consequence, crime is accelerated and increased by law. (ibid.: 32)

Heretofore, young Black boys and girls were treated the same as adult offenders in the criminal justice system in the absence of proper intervention facilities. The filling of this void, according to the supporters of juvenile reformatories, could serve as a safety net for some Black youth who would, possibly, otherwise become hardened criminals in the absence of such a support system.

The eighth resolution commended Blacks for improving their social, economic and physical condition in the United States post enslavement. Specifically, beneficial and insurance societies, businesses, churches and secret societies were recognized for their works. The executive committee asserted that tremendous strides had been made, but more should be done along those lines by the educated and 'comfortable classes' of Blacks.

The ninth resolution asserted that the death rate for Blacks remained too high and that Blacks should be taught the importance of health and hygiene. For example, in Charleston, South Carolina the death rate per 1,000 for scrofula and syphilis in 1896 was .40 for Whites and 7.77 for Blacks. Additionally, the regular death rate per 1,000 city residents for Charleston during the same period was 21.10 for Whites and 40.32 for Blacks. These data were collected for the 1896 and 1897 investigations and were included in the 1898 publication because of its incompleteness at the time of printing for those conference reports.

Although Du Bois served as the lead researcher and editor of the 1898 Atlanta University study and publication, the topic for this investigation was chosen by George G. Bradford prior to Du Bois's arrival. The next 15 publications reflect Du Bois's vision and methodological rigor that resulted in the establishment of the first American School of sociology.

Atlanta University Publication #4, 1899
"The Negro in Business"
Edited by W. E. B. Du Bois

The "Negro in Business" was the topic of the 1899 investigation, conference and publication. This inquiry followed Du Bois's plan of investigating, annually, a specific problem concerning Blacks in America as opposed to George G. Bradford's plan of investigating a hodgepodge of city problems each year. The major objective of this investigation was to ascertain the total number and different types of Black owned business in various cities across the nation.

The primary methods of data collection were schedules and 1890 census data. Schedules, another name for questionnaire, were used to obtain information including the names of businesspersons and their companies, location, kind of business, number of years in business and the amount of capital amassed by each business. Schedules were mailed to Black businesspersons around the country and responses were received from 1,906 people representing 30 states.

This investigation, similar to the previous year's effort, included citizen researchers, many of whom had participated in the previous investigations. The benefit of repeatedly utilizing the same citizen researchers was that it continually, and theoretically, reduced the possibility of error had a new group of citizen researchers been used. The schedules were limited in nature and "care [was] taken to make the questions few in number, simple and direct, and, so far as possible, incapable of misapprehension" (Du Bois 1899: 4) since researchers were relying on the businesspersons to serve as *de facto* social scientists. The schedules were mailed to "well-educated Negroes, long resident in the communities; by calling on the same persons for aid year after year, a body of experienced correspondents has been gradually formed, numbering now about fifty" (ibid.: 4).

The validity of the data gathered for this investigation, as in previous studies, was grounded in the honesty of the citizen researcher. Commenting on the use of insider researchers, Du Bois argued that the data collected "represent, therefore, the reports of businessmen themselves, interpreted and commented upon by an intelligent investigator of some experience. [The data collected] can, therefore, on the whole, be depended upon as substantially accurate" (ibid.: 5). Although Du Bois believed the data, in general, to be accurate, he admitted "the item of 'capital invested' is naturally apt to contain the largest amount of errors since it is in most cases an estimate" (ibid.: 5). Thus, capital invested estimates and others deemed too high were removed from the data and the resolutions of the conference reflected the necessary adjustments.

The first resolution encouraged Blacks "to enter into business life in increasing numbers. The present disproportion in the distribution of Negroes in the various occupations," according to the executive committee, "is unfortunate" (ibid.: 50). They argued that "a one-sided development, unnecessarily increases competition in certain lines of industry, and puts the mass of Negro people out of sympathy and touch with the industrial and mercantile spirit of the age" (ibid.: 50). Miss Hattie G. Escridge, a member of the Atlanta Sociological Laboratory, examined 1890 census data and concluded, "All the young people who are graduating from our schools to-day, cannot be school teachers and preachers" (ibid.: 61) and some should be instructed to take the extra step to become businesspersons. Thus, the pigeon holing of Blacks into limited professions would be offset with their entry into other professions including barbering, blacksmithing and farming, where they could become entrepreneurs and provide opportunities for the next generation of Blacks.

In the second resolution it was proposed that "we need as merchants the best trained young men we can find. A college training ought to be one of the best preparations for a broad business life; and thorough English and high school training is indispensable" (ibid.: 50). This proposition was offered because an educated workforce, especially managerial staff, could reduce the amount of mismanagement that Atlanta University researchers found to exist in many businesses. The executive committee proposed that the grocery store market was fertile ground for mismanagement or exploitation. Records indicated that, out of 25 Black grocery store owners investigated in 1898, only one had college training, nine had common school training, 12 could only read and write and three had no education at all. That these persons possessed little to no formal education, according to the executive committee, could lead to the mismanagement of the financial matters of the businesses investigated.

The third resolution recommended that Black businesspersons "remember that their customers demand courtesy, honesty, and careful methods, and they should not expect patronage when their manner of conducting business does not justify it" (ibid.: 50). This resolution extended from the observations of various citizen researchers who witnessed businesspersons not being courteous to some of their patrons.

The fourth resolution encouraged Blacks to support Black owned businesses such that the revenues garnered from the members of their community circulated through and remained inside their community. Miss Hattie G. Escridge, an 1898 Atlanta University graduate herself, strongly supported this idea and asserted that:

> By Negroes sticking together and spending whatever they have to spend with their own race soon they would be able to unite and open large, up-to-date, dry-goods, millinery, hardware and all other establishments as run by their white brothers, thereby giving employment to those who have nothing to do … The Negro has helped to make rich every race on earth but his own. They will walk three blocks or more to trade with a white man, when there is a Negro store next to their door. They say the Negro does not have as good material as the white man. In all cases that is not true, for they have bought from the same wholesale grocer and have the same material … We have aided the Jew from the time he came into our neighborhood with his store on his back … until now he has a large brick building, a number of clerks, and he and family ride in a fine carriage drawn by expensive horses, and they driven by a Negro. Why can we not help our brother who is struggling with all the odds against him, and has been since the day of his birth. (ibid.: 61)

The fifth resolution congratulated and recognized the 1,906 businesspersons who returned their questionnaires to conference officials. Their efforts were duly noted in the official records of the conference and their assistance on future investigations was proposed. The sixth, and final, resolution encouraged young boys and girls to become businesspersons, promoted the notion that thrift and savings be encouraged among Blacks and recommended that a *Negro Business League* be established in every American city to guide and support Black business enterprises.

The 1899 investigation, conference and publication were the first in which Du Bois selected the topic and directed the entire research investigation. This project signaled the beginning of the Atlanta Sociological Laboratory's ascension to sociological excellence through its promotion of a rigorous methodology, data collection and keen analysis.

Atlanta University Publication #5, 1900
"The College-Bred Negro"
Edited by W. E. B. Du Bois

The topic of the 1900 investigation, conference and publication was "The College-Bred Negro." This investigation concerned, primarily, the "number, distribution, occupations, and success of College-bred Negroes" (Du Bois 1900: 5). These data were obtained by analyzing admissions data from various colleges and universities, letters received from White and Black college presidents concerning Black students and their progress, or lack thereof, and data received from Black college graduates themselves.

Data from this study indicated that 12 responses were received from college/university presidents as well as one from the United States Commissioner on Education concerning the number and ability of Black college students. College presidents responding to this inquiry included those representing Amherst College, Boston University, Bowdoin College, Harvard College, the University of Indiana, the University of Iowa, the University of Michigan and Yale University. Data were also received from 1,312 African American college graduates. Information concerning their occupation, group leadership activities, political activity and ownership of private and public property were analyzed. These data were used to ascertain the state of the education of Blacks at the turn of the twentieth century.

No resolutions were offered in this research investigation as the emphasis was largely on ascertaining the number and occupations of Black college graduates. Despite the limited scope of this inquiry, Du Bois believed "the central truth which this study teaches to the candid mind is the success of higher education under the limitations and difficulties of the past" (ibid.: 32).

Atlanta University Publication #6, 1901
"The Negro Common School"
Edited by W. E. B. Du Bois

The subject of the 1901 Atlanta University investigation, conference and publication concerned the condition and status of "The Negro Common

School." This study emanated from the previous year's investigation which uncovered data indicating that 53 percent of Black college graduates were employed as teachers. Upon learning this information Atlanta University officials decided to study, more intensely, the Black common (or public) school to ascertain its effect on the social and economic condition of Blacks in America. The methods of data collection used in this investigation were the examination of school reports from several states, reports from the Freedmen's Bureau and the United States Bureau of Education, three sets of blanks distributed in various school districts and returns from numerous teachers.

School reports were received from 16, mostly southern, states and the District of Columbia concerning the total number of school age children, illiteracy rates, amount of money appropriated by each state for White and Black schools, amount of school taxes paid, salary information, attendance and per capita expenditure for Black and White schools. Reports from the Freedmen's Bureau and the United States Bureau of Education provided data relative to the total number of Blacks working as common school teachers, their age and sex and other demographic information.

Three sets of blanks were mailed to subjects participating in this investigation. The first set of blanks represented data received from various county and city superintendents throughout the United States. Questions asked of these individuals included employee history of Black workers, efforts at social betterment supported by various schools, the strengths and weaknesses of Black teachers, wages of White and Black teachers and a performance comparison between Black and White teachers. According to conference data, 42 responses were received from county superintendents and 34 responses were received from city superintendents. The second and third sets of blanks represented data received from principals of various Black southern city and town schools. Questions asked of these individuals concerned the employee history of Black workers, wages of White and Black teachers, the attitudes of city officials toward Black schools, school maintenance, needs of the school and the strengths and weaknesses of Black teachers.

The final method of data collection consisted of questionnaires received from 16 county school teachers located in various regions of the South. These teachers offered information concerning their experiences with Black students, the impact of college education on the lives of their Black students and the occupations they encouraged students to enter. Data received from these sources were analyzed to note similarities and differences based upon characteristics such as location and gender. The exact location of the teachers participating in this investigation was not provided; however, researchers intimated that the sample consisted primarily of southern subjects. The combination of the data collection techniques cited above formed the basis for the resolutions offered in this study.

The first resolution called for an increase in state and national aid for Black high schools. Data collected for this study revealed that state monies allotted for the maintenance and running of Black schools was less than that of comparable White schools. The state of Delaware, in 1896 for example, exhausted $1.66 per capita for each White student while only spending $0.81 for its Black students. While the situation of Blacks in Delaware was distasteful as they were responsible for the partial financial support of their schools, they fared better than their peers in the American South. In Arkansas, South Carolina, Georgia, Alabama, Mississippi and Louisiana, Blacks were solely responsible for securing the costs associated with running their schools. Atlanta University researchers reported that if monies were not provided by Blacks to support their public schools then they were forced to close. In addition to inequality in the funding of public schools, Atlanta University officials discovered discrepancies in teacher salaries. For example, in 1898 Maryland paid its White teachers $8.76 while Black teachers received $4.07. The lack of equal funding for public schools and the disparity in pay between White and Black teachers fueled the executive committee's call for increased state and national funding for Black schools.

The second resolution called for "increased interest, effort, and sacrifice for an education on the part of the Negroes themselves" (Du Bois 1901: ii). Conference officials believed that increased support from Blacks could result in additional funding for their schools. Additionally, conference officials ardently believed that an increase in the level of education among Blacks would lead to improved racial, social and economic conditions.

As indicated earlier, the major goal of this investigation was to ascertain the exact condition of Black schools. Conference data revealed Black schools to be in dire need of financial support and that Blacks were employed as teachers in high numbers because other employment opportunities were blocked to them. This revelation provoked Du Bois to assert that:

> If carpenters are needed it is well and good to train men as carpenters; if teachers are needed it is well and good to train men as teachers. But to train men as carpenters and then set them to teaching is wasteful and criminal; and to train men as teachers and then refuse them living wages unless they become carpenters is rank nonsense. (ibid.: 117)

Atlanta University Publication #7, 1902
"The Negro Artisan"
Edited by W. E. B. Du Bois

The 1902 investigation, conference and publication focused on the status of Black artisans. An artisan was defined as "a skilled laborer—a person who works with his hands but has attained a degree of skill and efficiency above that of an ordinary manual laborer—as, for instance, carpenters, masons, engineers, blacksmiths, etc. Omit barbers, ordinary laborers in factories, who do not do skilled work, etc" (Du Bois 1902: 9). In this investigation Atlanta University researchers attempted to identify the various occupations of Blacks beyond the profession of education where the majority of Blacks found themselves employed.

The data collection techniques used were secondary analysis, questionnaires, schedules, correspondences and a collaborative investigation with a Tennessee newspaper, the *Chattanooga Tradesman*. Additional data were collected from the Conservative Review, Freedmen's Bureau, Hampton University Negro Conference, United States Census Bureau and the United States Department of Labor. Information gathered from these outlets enabled researchers to identify the number and exact location of Black artisans in the United States.

One-thousand three-hundred questionnaires were sent to skilled laborers, mostly in the state of Georgia, who were identified by Atlanta University graduates and other citizens of note. In their attempt to make this study as reliable as possible, Atlanta University researchers compared data received from workers of the same company to identify substantive differences in their responses. Also, responses received from employees were compared to responses received from their employer. For example, data received from worker A were compared with data received from worker B of the same company. This was done to insure that the responses did not vary greatly. The same data requested from workers were also solicited from employers. The collection of data from worker A, worker B and their employer provided a data collection technique by which the information received were reliable and the possibility of inaccuracy reduced. Questions asked of employees and employers concerned the wages of Black employees, comparison of work habits between Whites and Blacks, education level of Black employees and any information concerning the practices of local unions.

Questionnaires were mailed to "every trade union affiliated with the American Federation of Labor and all others that could be reached" (ibid.: 10). Researchers amassed 97 responses with 11 unions choosing not to respond after multiple requests. The information sought concerned the number of Blacks in each union, possible refusal of Black applicants into the organization, work habits of Black workers and their general opinion of Black artisans.

Two-hundred responses were received from various "central labor bodies in every city and town of the Union" (ibid.: 10). These data came from 30 states and the questions centered on Black membership in the union, discrimination against Black members, work habits of Blacks and the overall ability of Black workers.

In addition to the questionnaires that were mailed to skilled laborers, trade unions and central labor bodies, a "schedule was placed in the hands of correspondents of this Conference-mostly College-bred Negroes and professional men-and they were asked to study their particular communities. Reports were received from 32 states, besides Ontario, Costa Rica, and Porta Rica" (ibid.: 9). Data received from schedules centered on the number of skilled artisans in each community, type of jobs held by each artisan, amount of work managed by the artisans, effect of industrial school training on the artisan, amount of discrimination experienced, the ability, or lack thereof, of Blacks to join unions and a brief history of Black artisans in the community was requested.

Letters were mailed to industrial schools seeking information pertaining to the occupation and location of their graduates, some of the difficulties graduates often met in finding employment, union affiliation and a list of graduates was requested. In addition to the data cited above, "to the state and federations a letter was sent asking for whatever general information was not available on the subject" (ibid.: 11).

Last, Atlanta University and the *Chattanooga Tradesman* collaborated to conduct a study on Black artisans in the South. The *Chattanooga Tradesman* conducted similar investigations in 1889 and 1891. Hence, the plan for the 1902 investigation was to replicate and expand the previous studies. The data collection methods for this investigation included questionnaires that were delivered to the employers of Black artisans, southern educators and public school children. Also, United States census reports and reports from the Bureau of Education were utilized.

Information obtained from employers concerned the number of Black employees and their skill level, wages, comparison of work habits to White workers, level and effect of education on Blacks and the employers' willingness to employ Black artisans in the future. Researchers also wanted to determine the types of vocational training offered to Blacks. In order to obtain this information, "the Superintendents of Education in all Southern States were consulted as to Manual training in the schools, and most of them answered the inquiries" (ibid.: 12). Last, a questionnaire was presented to 600 public school children in Atlanta, Georgia. Questions focused on the kind of work the children completed at home, the availability and use of hammers and saws at home, identification of their best talent and what they wanted to become when they grew up. The final method of data collection was the secondary analysis of census and education reports. The thorough triangulation of data collection techniques employed for this investigation resulted in it being the school's most scientifically sound endeavor to date. Atlanta University officials readily acknowledged:

Finally such available information was collected as could be found in the United States' census, the reports of the Bureau of Education, and other sources as indicated in the bibliography. On the whole the collected information on which this study is based is probably more complete than in the case of any previous studies. (ibid.: 12)

The first resolution stressed the need for Blacks to increase the prestige of skilled artisan occupations. According to conference officials, "concerted action and intelligent preparation would before long restore and increase the prestige of skilled Negro working men" (ibid.: 7). To date, occupations in fields such as education, medicine and religion were highly valued and everything else was viewed as inferior. Conference officials asserted that skilled labor should be promoted just as vigorously among Blacks, young and old, as a desirable occupation.

The second resolution called for the continuation of Black participation in the artisan areas already entered and for Blacks to enter areas where their numbers were low or nonexistent. 1890 census data revealed that Black artisans were over-represented in areas such as masonry and carpentry and under-represented as machinists and wheelwrights. Conference officials urged Blacks to enter the areas in which they had little or no representation and, thus, decrease competition in saturated areas while establishing businesses in new areas of need.

The third resolution requested that all trade and labor unions admit Black workers and end all discriminatory actions aimed at Blacks once admitted. For example, "The prejudiced element prevailed, however, at the last meeting in Boston, 1902, of the Stationary Engineers and it was voted to have the word 'white' placed before the word 'engineers' in one of the articles of their constitution" (ibid.: 165). Researchers discovered that almost all Black artisans in the United States were omitted from union participation. Responding to these data, Atlanta University officials suggested that a union can only be as strong as its most silenced members. Thus, omitting Blacks from membership was detrimental not only to the social and economic well-being of Black workers, but to the economic well-being of poor and working class White workers as well. If the two groups remained separated by race then employers could use the pool of Black artisans as a means to drive down the total wages of all workers. This was a possibility that the executive committee pushed back against in a very stern manner as the implementation of such an agenda would be harmful to both Black and White workers.

The fourth resolution commended the training of Blacks in trade schools. Data obtained from various trade schools indicated that "the movements in this line, especially in the last ten years, have been of estimable benefit to the freedmen's sons" (ibid.: 8).

The fifth resolution called for the establishment of industrial settlements for Blacks. It was hoped that "the industrial settlements of Negroes ... would offer peculiarly promising fields of enterprise for a philanthropy based on solid business principles" (ibid.: 8).

The sixth resolution requested help from public schools, agencies for the social betterment of Blacks and colleges in advancing the ranks of Black artisans. "We insist that no permanent advance in industrial or other lines can be made without three great indirect helps" (ibid.: 8). This plea was made with the understanding that the social uplift of Blacks must include representatives from the entire American society; not just a few.

The 1902 Atlanta University study is noteworthy because it fully embodies Du Bois's plan of rigorous scholarly inquiry through the use of triangulation. The result was, arguably, the most methodologically sound of any Atlanta University study. This prototype of sociological inquiry would serve as the ideal model for subsequent investigations.

Atlanta University Publication #8, 1903
"The Negro Church"
Edited by W. E. B. Du Bois

"The Negro Church" was the subject of the 1903 investigation, conference and publication. This topic was chosen because Atlanta University officials wanted to ascertain the "religion of Negroes and its influence on their moral habits" (Du Bois 1903: v). The methods of data collection included secondary data analysis, special reports, questionnaires and a review of the existing literature.

1890 United States census data were used to identify the religious affiliations of Blacks. Additionally, financial and membership information were solicited from the annual conferences of the A. M. E. Z. Church, A. M. E. Church, C. M. E. Church, M. E. Church and the National Baptist Convention. The special reports utilized in this investigation included 250 responses from pastors and other church officials, 175 from Black laypersons, 117 from the heads of schools of prominent men (White and Black), 54 from Southern White persons, 13 from Black theological schools and 109 from northern theological schools. All of these special reports contained data on the morality of Blacks in America.

Questionnaires were administered to 1,300 school children in Richmond, VA, Chicago, IL, Atlanta, GA, Deland, FL, Thomas County, GA and Greene County, OH. Children were asked questions such as "Are you a Christian?," "Do you go to church?," "Why do you like a certain church the best?," and "What does it mean to be a Christian?" The questions were designed to determine the level of religiosity of the children and to note possible similarities and differences when comparing socio-economic differences.

The final data collection source was the existing literature on religion. *Religious Life in America* by Ernest H. Abbott (1902) and *Christianity, Islam, and the Negro Race* by Edward W. Blyden (1887) are representative samples of the voluminous literature on religion reviewed by Atlanta University researchers.

The data collected for this investigation resulted in one resolution that called for the "strengthening of ideals of life and living" (ibid.: 207) among Blacks. Atlanta University officials, similar to previous publications, specifically identified Black women as the individuals charged with leading the much needed spiritual revolution of the race. Additionally, conference officials stressed the need for Black women to be protected from sexual terrorism at the hands of White men. To this end, Atlanta University officials asserted that "upon the *women* of no race have the truths of the gospel taken a firmer and deeper hold than upon the colored women of the United States. For her protection and by her help a religious rebirth is needed" (ibid.: 207).

Atlanta University Publication #9, 1904
"Some Notes on Negro Crime Particularly in Georgia"
Edited by W. E. B. Du Bois

The subject of the 1904 investigation, conference and publication was "Negro Crime in Georgia." This study was initially conceptualized to cover the extent of crime committed by Blacks on a national scale. However, because "The whole discussion of crime in the United States has usually been based on the census returns, and these are very inadequate" (Du Bois 1904: v), conference officials decided to gather as much accurate data as possible in the state of Georgia in the hope of having some accurate and scientific data on the subject in lieu of their inability to capture a national sample. Atlanta University researchers openly acknowledged, "These data are less complete than in the case of our previous studies and few conclusions can be drawn until further facts and figures are available" (ibid.: v). Despite these limitations, conference officials were confident that the methods of data collection used in this study provided essential information concerning crime in Georgia and, by extension, the South. Data for this study were drawn from analyses of special studies of court returns and other data from Atlanta and Savannah, reports from mayors, chiefs of police and other officers in 37 Georgia counties, reports from Black and White citizens in 37 Georgia counties, police data from 20 United States cities, seven reports of the Georgia Prison Commission and questionnaires distributed to 2,000 school-aged children.

Court returns and other judicial data from Atlanta and Savannah were used to discover the total number of arrests and convictions of Blacks, compare arrest records between Black males and females and Blacks and Whites, and to discover the ages of offenders and other demographic information. Special reports were received from every chief of police in the state of Georgia as well as responses from various county officials and White citizens. The data provided by these individuals revealed their knowledge of the amount of crime committed by Blacks, the increase or decrease of crime committed by Blacks in recent years and any additional remarks that they wanted to offer on this topic. Reports were also solicited from Black residents of Georgia concerning the types of crime committed, the fairness or unfairness of the justice system and the condition of the Georgia prison system.

Arrest rates from cities such as New York, NY, Philadelphia, PA, Washington D.C., Cincinnati, OH and Louisville, KY were used to chart possible increases and/or decreases in the crimes of Blacks on a national level and to identify any contrast between the number and or type of arrests made by region. These data were also used to elicit information about the wrongful and lengthy imprisonment of Blacks under the unscrupulous Jim Crow American judicial system. Data from the Georgia Prison Commission were used, in part, to verify the existence and extent of the convict lease system. The convict lease system, a precursor of the contemporary prison industrial complex, was an arrangement whereby, for example, the state of Georgia would lease the labor of its prisoners to private companies for a profit garnered by the government. Data supplied by the Georgia Prison Commission cited the number and types of jobs that prisoners were assigned, length of prison sentences and the amount of money received by the state for the lease agreement.

Questionnaires were administered to 2,000 school children. The questionnaires sought to answer the question of 'what Negroes think of crime.' Children between the ages 9 and 15 were asked questions concerning the purpose of laws, what they believed the primary function of the court system to be, and whether or not all people convicted of crimes were bad and guilty. These questions were designed to ascertain why, from the perspective of a child, individuals engage in deviant behavior.

Although Atlanta University officials acknowledged the incompleteness of their project, they were confident that the resolutions offered could be used as a starting point for understanding the conditions surrounding the criminal justice system, policing and Black Americans. The first resolution acknowledged that a large amount of crime was being committed by Blacks in Georgia. For example, arrest records from Atlanta and Savannah, during the years 1898–1903, indicated that Blacks were convicted of crimes at twice the level of their White peers.

The second resolution asserted that the causes of the high rates of crime were the inability of Blacks to make the smooth transition from slavery to freedom, racial prejudice, less legal protection under the law, especially for Black women, race specific laws, white court justice and Black court injustice and because the methods of punishment bred more crime. Highlighting the first part of this resolution, the executive committee asserted that "The mass of Negroes are in a transient stage between slavery and freedom. Such a period of change involves physical strain, mental bewilderment, and moral weakness. Such periods of stress have among all people given rise to crime and a criminal class" (ibid.: 65).

The third resolution suggested that the amount of crime committed by Blacks, while high, was not on the increase in Georgia. In fact, between 1895 and 1904 they noted a substantial decrease in the total number of Blacks convicted of crime in Georgia.

The fourth resolution posited that "the cure for Negro crime lies in moral uplift and inspiration among Negroes" (ibid.: 65). This resolution extended from the previous year's study on the Black church wherein it was proposed that the entire community would benefit from a spiritual awakening that would, hopefully, lead to increased morality and decreased levels of crime.

The fifth resolution appealed to Whites for fairer criminal laws, justice in the courts, abolition of the convict lease system, more intelligent methods of punishment, refusal to allow free labor to be displaced by convict labor and the acknowledgment that it was the *lower classes* of people who were threats to the citizens of Georgia, not necessarily all Blacks. This *appeal to Whites* appears to have been a class based attempt by the educated grade of Blacks to repudiate theories suggesting that biological factors led to an over-representation of Blacks as criminals and convicts.

The 1904 Atlanta University study, while emphasizing the experiences of Blacks in Georgia, was, at a minimum, regionally generalizable as researchers uncovered data identifying specific institutional injustices experienced by Blacks in the South that had, heretofore, been viewed as hearsay or myth, or cast as sporadic occurrences. The physical violence and disfranchisement of Blacks in this era of Jim Crow was exposed. The precursor to today's problematic practice of prison privatization, the convict lease system, was also exposed in this publication. Although the civil rights of Blacks were not fully granted and protected in this nation until the middle of the twentieth century, this investigation, while documenting the existence of social inequality against Blacks, can be viewed as an early scientific strike at forcing Americans to recognize the problematic nature of the policing of Blacks and Black communities and the need for the strengthening of laws promoting the legal protection of Blacks from Whites.

Atlanta University Publication #10, 1905
"A Select Bibliography of the Negro American"
Edited by W. E. B. Du Bois

The tenth Atlanta University publication contained only a bibliography of the existing literature on Blacks in the United States. This endeavor was not the first attempt at such a bibliography. "A first modest attempt at a short bibliography was made in a four-page leaflet. Published in 1900. This was enlarged in a second edition (1901) to 9 pages. The present report is thus in a sense a third edition of this bibliography" (Du Bois 1905: 5). This bibliography was a useful tool for those desiring to identify the major scholarly works on Blacks at the turn of the century. The only resolution offered at this conference asserted that "the results of ten years' study of these social questions have justified the meetings and the methods of study employed" (ibid.: 7).

Atlanta University Publication #11, 1906
"The Health and Physique of the Negro American"
Edited by W. E. B. Du Bois

The 1906 investigation, conference and publication addressed the health and physique of Blacks in America. "This [investigation] marks the beginning of a second cycle of stud[ies] and takes up again the subject of the physical condition of Negroes, [first addressed in the 1896 and 1897 investigations], but enlarges the inquiry beyond the mere matter of mortality" (Du Bois 1906: 5). Data were obtained via reports from the United States census, reports of life insurance companies, vital records of cities and towns, reports of the United States Surgeon General, reports from Black hospitals and drug stores, reports from medical schools, letters from physicians, measurements of 1,000 Hampton University students and an examination of the general literature.

United States census data from the years 1790–1900 were utilized to obtain information concerning the geographic distribution of Blacks, increases or decreases in the Black population, mortality, causes of death and birth rates. Additionally, census data were used comparatively to determine the total number of United States citizens, their sex and age, number of 'defectives,' 'mulattoes,' and delinquents, and the causes and rates of mortality.

Reports of life insurance companies were examined to identify the "distribution of the economic burden" (ibid.: 91) carried by these organizations. The perceived economic burden of insuring Blacks had previously resulted in the denial of insurance to them based upon the assumption that their rates of death were higher than other groups. In response to this unfounded position, Atlanta University researchers produced data suggesting a different conclusion.

The reports of the 34 leading companies conclude: 'It has been supposedly in the past that colored people have less vitality than whites, but the somewhat scanty facts here available do not prove it.' In fact the Negro makes a better showing than the Irish, nearly as good as the Germans, and better than the economic class of laborers in general. To be sure these Negroes were carefully selected, but this fact only emphasizes the injustice which would have been done them had they been discriminated against merely on account of color, as the insurance companies so often do. (ibid.: 92)

The vital records of various cities and towns and reports of the United States Surgeon General were used to identify death rates, causes of death and the social conditions experienced by Blacks in cities such as New York, NY, Indianapolis, IN, Chicago, IL, Columbus, OH, Cleveland, OH, Memphis, TN, St. Louis, MO, Washington D.C., New Orleans, LA and Charleston, SC. Reports from Black hospitals and drug stores were used to identify institutions that accepted Blacks as patients, the total number of drug stores in 25 states, the total number of dentists and pharmacists in the nation, capital held by these institutions and the number of workers employed. "A circular was sent to all [of] the medical schools in the country, asking if they had Negro students or graduates and [seeking information concerning] their character, etc." (ibid.: 98). Reports were received from 23 White medical colleges. Questionnaires were also mailed to various Black physicians to identify their current location and place of graduation. As of 1906, the primary institutions charged with training Black physicians were Meharry Medical College (Nashville), Howard University Medical Department (Washington D.C.), Leonard Medical School (Raleigh, N.C.), Flint Medical College (New Orleans) and Louisville National Medical College (Louisville).

About 1,000 students from Hampton University participated in this study by allowing researchers to measure their head and cranio-facial skeletons, describe their racial types and obtain other descriptive and physical data that could be used in comparison with White Americans. The purpose of this study was to dispel various myths concerning the supposed physical and biological differences between Blacks and Whites. Additionally, the data collected were used to catalogue intragroup differences between Blacks based upon skin tone and other physical characteristics. The combination of these data collection techniques produced findings that debunked various myths concerning the health and physique of Blacks in the United States.

The first resolution suggested that the overall health of Blacks was improving. Data indicated lower rates of overall death and infant mortality, and decreased deaths from tuberculosis than were discovered in the 1896 and 1897 studies. Overall, the data collected for this study showed a marked decline in the total number of deaths from these conditions. The second resolution insisted that, despite a drop in the death rate for Blacks, their mortality rate remained too high when compared to other racial groups. To this end, the executive committee recommended the formation of local health leagues to address the health concerns and needs of Blacks. The third resolution argued that special effort was needed to end tuberculosis in the Black community. As indicated earlier, the death rate due to tuberculosis declined between 1896 and 1906. Nevertheless, Atlanta University researchers asserted that Blacks needed additional assistance in conquering the disease because they continued to be disproportionately affected. The fourth resolution found no evidence of the physical inferiority of Blacks when compared to Whites. This conclusion was reached through the voluntary efforts of the 1,000 Hampton University students who allowed their bodies to be used comparatively against the existing literature that heartily promoted scientific racism theories supporting the notion that Blacks were biologically and physically inferior to Whites.

The 1906 investigation embodied Du Bois's plan of systematic, objective and scientific inquiry as it challenged existing car window sociological analyses of Blacks that predominated the existing literature. The significance of this study is grounded in the fact that it provided data to contradict commonly accepted myths concerning Blacks in the medical community. While this study produced data debunking commonly believed theories of physical differences between Blacks and Whites (this topic is addressed fully in Chapter 3), upon its publication, and even today, the importance of this scholarly effort was not recognized. Dr. W. Montague Cobb, of Howard School of Medicine, placed the significance of the Du Bois-led 1906 effort into context when he stated:

> [This inquiry was the first] significant scientific approach to the health problems and biological study of the Negro … But,' said Cobb, 'neither the Negro medical profession nor the Negro educational world was ready for it. Its potential usefulness was not realized by Negroes. Whites were hostile to such a study … This study, Du Bois's single excursion into the health field, was, said Cobb, 'an extraordinary forward pass heaved the length of the field, but there were no receivers.' (Du Bois 1968: vi)

Atlanta University Publication #12, 1907
"Economic Co-Operation among Negro Americans"
Edited by W. E. B. Du Bois

The 1907 investigation, conference and publication focused on the economic relationships established between Black businesses and "is a continuation and enlargement of [the 1898 conference, "Some Efforts of American Negroes for their Own Social Betterment"] made nearly ten years ago, with certain limitations and changes. The question set before us in the present study is: How far is there and has there been among Negro Americans a conscious effort at mutual aid in earning a living?" (Du Bois 1907: 10). Information concerning the origin of African entrepreneurial activities, the development of cooperative efforts among Blacks in America and the current types of economic cooperation were presented in this publication.

The methods of data collection used in this investigation were not as clearly defined as in previous studies. However, an examination of the appendix indicated that some data were collected via personal correspondences with businesspersons and social societies throughout the southern United States, conference reports citing economic data from various churches and an analysis of the existing literature. The data collected focused on the extent and types of economic cooperation between Black institutions such as the church, school, beneficial and insurance societies, banks, etc. From these sources a single resolution was offered by the executive committee: that "efforts should be made to foster and emphasize [the] present tendencies among Negroes toward co-operative effort and that the ideal of wide ownership of small capital and small accumulations among many rather than great riches among a few, should persistently be held before them" (ibid.: 4).

Conference officials suggested that economic cooperation, emanating from the church and extending into the private business world, was vital in an era where Blacks were disenfranchised economically and politically. Moreover, barely 40 years post emancipation, Atlanta University officials believed Blacks faced a critical crossroad that could determine the fate of the race.

> One way lead[s] to the old trodden ways of grasping fierce individualistic competition, where the shrewd, cunning, skilled, and rich among them will prey upon the ignorance and simplicity of the mass of the race and get wealth at the expense of the general well being; the other way leading to co-operation in capital and labor, the massing of small savings, the wide distribution of capital and a more general equality of wealth and comfort. (ibid.: 9)

The executive committee asserted that the best course of action for Blacks was the path leading to increased racial solidarity and, as stated in previous publications, reliance upon one other economically. This, Atlanta University officials posited, would result in the economic and political strengthening of the Black community.

Atlanta University Publication #13, 1908
"The Negro Family"
Edited by W. E. B. Du Bois

The 1908 investigation, conference and publication focused on 'The Negro Family.' This study was a continuation of previous investigations addressing family issues. For example:

> In 1897 the Atlanta University Negro Conference made an investigation into the 'Social and Physical Condition of Negroes in Cities,' which involved a study of 4742 individuals gathered in 1137 families, living in 59 different groups, in 18 different cities. These data were compiled by the United States Department of Labor and published in Bulletin number ten; and, as the editor said, 'Great credit is due the investigators for their work.' The object of the investigation was to study the mortality of Negroes and the social and family conditions. The study of Mortality was continued in 1906 by Atlanta University publication number eleven. The present study continues the study of social conditions from the point of view of the family group. (Du Bois 1908: 5)

The methods of data collection used in this investigation included an examination of the existing slavery literature, United States Census Bureau reports, reports from the United States Bureau of Labor, previous Atlanta University studies and local investigations conducted by Atlanta University graduate and undergraduate students. Similar to previous investigations, Atlanta University officials acknowledged the limitations of their study and noted the dearth of existing and accurate data on the subject. Conference officials argued, "there is perhaps enough [data collected for this study] to give a tentative outline which more exact research may later fill in" (ibid.: 9).

The slavery literature was useful as it provided data concerning the structure and organization of the Black family during that period of American history. Some of the slavery era data collected (i.e., personal narratives and diaries) were utilized to assess the structure and organization of African tribes prior to European contact. Overall, this data source helped identify the types of social and familial relations that existed among people of African descent before and immediately after the introduction of kidnapped Africans into the Americas.

Census reports of 1890 and 1900 were used to gain demographic information such as the size of the Black population in each state, the number of Blacks by age and sex, conjugal conditions, number of farms and homes owned, employment status, etc. Additionally, previous Atlanta University studies, specifically the 1897 and 1906 investigations, were used as sources of demographic and qualitative data concerning particular characteristics of Black families.

Eight reports of the United States Bureau of Labor were analyzed to gain information on the working condition of Blacks in various cities. The data, garnered through the use of schedules, were collected by Atlanta University graduates or citizen researchers who either resided in the particular location investigated or traveled to certain locations to gather data. All of the data contained in the reports were combined to assess the experiences faced by working class Blacks in various geographic locations. The collection of employment data assisted researchers in assessing the economic condition of families in Farmville, VA, the Black belt (e.g., Mississippi, Alabama, Tennessee), Sandy Spring, MD, an unspecified county in the state of Georgia, Litwalton, VA, Cinclaire Central Factory and Calumet Plantation, LA and Xenia, OH.

Sixteen Atlanta University students supplemented the data identified above with their own research investigation. As part of their academic requirement, the college classes of 1909 and 1910 investigated the social and familial conditions of 32 families in Atlanta. These students walked door-to-door in various neighborhoods gathering data through the use of schedules. The information collected by Atlanta University students was combined with the aforementioned data to form a substantial collection of information about the Black family in that area.

Similar to previous investigations, Atlanta University officials were aware of their lack of accurate and complete data. Despite its limitations, Du Bois asserted that data collected for this study were:

> Based on first-hand knowledge, and are unusually accurate. They do not, however, represent properly the proportion of different types among the mass of Negroes. Most of the families studied belong to the upper half of the black population. Finally, to repeat, this study is but a sketch with no pretense toward attempting to exhaust a fruitful subject. The main cause of its limitation is lack of material. (Ibid.: 9–10)

In spite of the limitations identified above, the executive committee offered three resolutions.

The first resolution instructed older Black women to teach young women "to appreciate the seriousness of marriage, its solemn import and its sacred responsibilities" (ibid.: 153). This resolution was offered in light of data that revealed high rates of 'illegitimate' births and female headed households. The answer to these problems, as suggested in previous studies, fell on the shoulders of Black women since they were expected to be the ones to champion morality for the race. The second resolution suggested that young men be taught to revere womanhood and motherhood "so that their purity may be no mere prudential restraint, but a generous and chivalrous Christian knightliness" (ibid.: 153). The third resolution emphasized that marriage and family were sacred institutions and should be treated as such. All of these resolutions extended from data indicating the virtual mockery of Black marriage during slavery, low levels of marriage for Blacks in 1890 and 1900, high rates of 'illegitimate births,' and, in some cases, complete disregard for the sanctity of marriage as evidenced by the existence of broken families resulting from "the abnormal number of widowed and separated, and the late age of marriage [that result in] sexual irregularity and economic pressure" (ibid.: 31).

The 1909 investigation, arguably, represents the first scholarly sociological study of the family in the United States. Notwithstanding Lewis H. Morgan's book, *League of the Iroquois* (1851), Rutledge M. Dennis is more effusive in his assessment of this investigation's place in sociological lore when it is included as part of a triumvirate with Du Bois's *Philadelphia Negro* and Farmville, VA study. According to Dennis (1975: 106), "Du Bois' 1908 study, *The Negro American Family*, was the first study of the sociology of family in the United States." That this study of the American family comprised the first of its kind in the United States, yet, neither the scholars who conducted the research nor the product itself are recognized in the literature, introductory textbooks in sociology, or sociology of the family textbooks is mindboggling and speaks volumes about the sociological invisibility this school has endured for more than 100 years. The invisibility of this school is addressed more fully in Chapter 4.

Atlanta University Publication #14, 1909
"Efforts for Social Betterment among Negro Americans"
Edited by W. E. B. Du Bois

The 1909 investigation, conference and publication were a continuation of the 1898 study titled "Efforts of American Negroes for their Own Social Betterment." The main objective of this project, similar to the initial investigation, was to ascertain the number and type of programs and activities designed to improve the social condition and morale of American Blacks. Similar to previous studies, Atlanta University officials readily acknowledged the limitations of their study. Officials stated, "it is ... again not possible to make an exhaustive study of Social Betterment among the ten million people of Negro descent in the United States. An attempt has been made, however, to secure in all parts of the country a fairly representative list of typical efforts and institutions, and the resulting picture while incomplete is nevertheless instructive" (Du Bois 1909: 5). The data collection techniques used in this investigation included questionnaires, census data and reports from various benevolence oriented organizations.

The questionnaire used in this investigation was designed to accumulate information concerning the charitable activities of various organizations devoted to the social uplift of Blacks. This objective was achieved by mailing letters "in all the chief centers of [the] Negro population [to] a number of persons of standing" (ibid.: 9). The letter requested that each recipient identify all charitable institutions, clubs, and/or organizations in their community and that they return the questionnaire to Atlanta University when completed. Once these data were received, letters were then mailed to the various charitable institutions, clubs and organizations identified. Data collected centered on the history of the organizations contacted, material facts of the group, pictures of buildings and members, economic data, examples of activities supported for the purpose of social uplift and the amount of property owned. Despite the absence of an accurate recording of the total number of reports received from the various organizations, study records revealed that "a large number of reports were obtained" (ibid.: 9) and they comprised the data supporting the resolutions of the conference.

The first resolution, a reaffirmation of a resolution presented in an earlier publication, insisted that Black churches become more institutional and reformatory while employing social workers. Data best reflective of this resolution and procured at the 1898 Atlanta University Conference suggested that:

> The Negro Church is the only social institution of the Negroes which started in the forests and survived slavery; under the leadership of the priest and medicine man, afterward of the Christian pastor, the Church preserved itself the remnants of Negro social life. So that to-day the Negro population of the United States is virtually divided into Church congregations, which are the real units of the race life. It is natural, therefore, that charitable and rescue work among Negroes should first be found in the churches and reach there its greatest development. (Du Bois 1898: 16)

This resolution was a continuation of the executive committee's challenge to the church to bear the institutional brunt of uplifting American Blacks because of its extensive history and longevity as the only African institution to survive the institution of slavery.

The second resolution requested that Black public schools be supported with government monies. The discrepancy in the level of funding for Black and White public schools was noted in the 1901 study, "The Negro Common School". For example, although Blacks comprised 35 percent of the students in Virginia, 33 percent in North Carolina and 46 percent in Georgia, only 14,

13, and 17 percent of the total cost of African American schools were funded by each respective state government.

The third resolution championed the establishment of additional women's clubs in each Black community for the express purpose of engaging in charitable programming. This resolution was offered in response to data revealing the extraordinary accomplishments of many women's clubs. For example:

> The White Rose Mission of New York city, organized about twenty years ago by Mrs Victoria Earle Matthews, has done much good work in that city. A large number of needy ones have found shelter within its doors and have been able to secure work of all kinds. This club has a committee to meet the incoming steamers from the South and see that young women entering the city as strangers are directed to proper homes. Mrs. Frances Keyser, who has charge of this work, is the right woman in the right place. (Du Bois 1909: 62)

The fourth resolution advocated the establishment of 'old folks homes,' orphanages and hospitals for Black Americans; a plea that was also made at a previous conference. Reports from Atlanta University researchers indicated the need for such institutions in cities such as Memphis, TN, St. Louis, MO and Winston-Salem, NC. These and many other cities had few, if any, institutions established to meet the various needs of the Black population in the cities investigated.

The fifth resolution insisted that organizations within the Black community engage in "work of rescue among women and children especially and also among men and boys is greatly needed, particularly among city Negroes, and has been neglected too long" (ibid.: 133). Thus, organizations such as the Young Men's and Women's Christian Associations, as well as refuges and rescue homes for women, were encouraged to participate in this endeavor.

The sixth resolution encouraged additional artistic training for Black youth. Data from various social, literary and art clubs in cities such as Houston, TX, Washington D.C., Dallas, TX and Cleveland, OH indicated a dearth of artistic training for Blacks. Atlanta University officials suggested that instead of simply focusing on traditional vocational and technical training, a combination of artistic and holistic educational training should be encouraged.

The seventh resolution advocated the establishment of nurseries, social settlements and kindergartens for the children of working parents. Conference officials recognized the need for these services and contended, "There ought to be not only several in each city and town, but also in county districts" (ibid.: 119).

The eighth resolution asserted that Blacks should be allowed to express their political rights without being disenfranchised. The executive committee addressed this issue directly:

> While something can be accomplished by organizations for civic reform among Negroes themselves, yet so long as the race is deprived of the ballot it is impossible to make such organizations of the highest efficiency in any avenue of life, whether it be education, religion, work, or social reform; the impossibility of the Negro accomplishing the best work so long as he is kept in political serfdom is manifest even to the casual student. (ibid.: 133)

Atlanta University Publication #15, 1910
"The College-Bred Negro American"
Edited by W. E. B. Du Bois and Augustus Granville Dill

"In 1900 the Atlanta University Negro Conference made an investigation of the college graduates among Negro Americans. This study received widespread publicity and did much towards clearing up misapprehension in regard to educated colored people" (Du Bois and Dill 1910: 5). Ten years later the topic was revisited with the intention of identifying the total number of Blacks enrolled in college, the occupations of Black college graduates, the current curriculum of Black colleges, the attitudes of *other* colleges toward Blacks and the attitudes of various college and university presidents concerning Black students. The data collection methods included examinations of various college catalogues, letters from numerous college and university officials and reports from 800 Black college graduates.

The catalogues of 32 Black colleges and universities were analyzed to identify the specific requirements for admission, courses needed for graduation, number of graduates and current students, amount of time devoted to specific areas of study and general curriculum information. These data were gathered from 'First Grade Colored Colleges' such as Howard University, Fisk University, Atlanta University, Wiley, Leland, Virginia Union University, Clark College, Knoxville College, Spelman College, Claflin University and Atlanta Baptist College, as well as 21 additional Black institutions of higher learning.

Letters were mailed to the presidents of many PWIs seeking information concerning the number of Black students enrolled at their institutions and the academic performance of Black students vis-à-vis White students. Replies were received from over 35 institutions including Princeton University, Yale University, Union College (Nebraska), the University of North Dakota, South Dakota State College, Oberlin College, Oregon Agricultural College,

Des Moines College, the University of Nebraska, University of Kansas and the University of Iowa.

Questionnaires received from 800 Black American college graduates comprised the final data source for this study. The information requested from respondents included age, sex, marital status, number of children, early life training, education, degrees, current occupation, membership in learned societies, publications, public offices held, activity in charitable work, amount of land owned, value of property, plans on educating their children, chief hindrances and present philosophy regarding current condition of Blacks in the United States. All of the data collected via students, presidents and catalogs combined to form the foundation for the resolutions offered.

The first resolution, which was not grounded in any tangible data, suggested there was a demand for college-trained Blacks. This pronouncement was made, in part, because of the growing number of jobs created by industrialization and the belief that educated Blacks could secure employment in this area as the number of jobs was projected to outpace the number of available workers.

The second resolution reported that Black college graduates were gainfully employed. Data collected by Atlanta University researchers indicated that 85 percent of the 800 respondents were employed. Of that number, 54 percent worked in education, 20 percent were preachers, seven percent practiced medicine and four percent practiced law. This fact, according to Atlanta University officials, affirmed that "Negro graduates are at present, with few exceptions, usefully and creditably employed" (ibid.: 7) and dispelled the myth that college educated Blacks would be unable to find employment because of racial prejudice.

The third resolution argued for the holistic college training of Blacks. Data elicited from the catalogues of various American colleges and universities revealed that an enormous number of credit hours were devoted to ancient and modern languages. The executive committee suggested that the attention given to foreign languages be reduced and instruction in social science courses increased.

The fourth resolution proposed that each state in America establish a public college devoted primarily to the training of Black Americans. This resolution was presented because Atlanta University researchers discovered that many Black youth who desired to obtain an education were often forced to travel across several states simply to attend a college that would allow them admission. The establishment of an institution, albeit segregated, in each state would provide easier access for students desirous of attending school close to home.

The fifth resolution requested that "there should be every effort towards co-operation between colleges in the same locality, and towards avoidance of unnecessary duplication of work" (ibid.: 7). This resolution probably emerged from the fact that Atlanta University was geographically surrounded by other predominately Black institutions, namely Spelman College, Atlanta Baptist College, Morris Brown College and Clark College. It is reasonable to suggest that school officials noticed examples of program duplication and concluded that institutions of higher learning in close proximity to one another should engage in the more practical use of institutional resources by joining together in collaborative projects when possible.

The sixth resolution, also not grounded in tangible data, called for the establishment of additional Black public high schools in the South. Conference officials argued that the establishment of southern high schools would provide a means to properly prepare young Black Americans with the skills needed to survive in this society and to prepare them for the rigors of college.

The seventh resolution challenged Black colleges to strictly adhere to the admission requirements stated in their catalogs. This resolution emerged from data indicating subjective admissions practices by some institutions.

The eighth resolution argued for the reduction of Greek and Latin taught in Black colleges and universities and the ninth resolution, conversely, argued for an increase in the instruction of the natural sciences, English, history and sociology. These resolutions, as indicated earlier, were presented in light of data that revealed an extraordinary amount of foreign language requirements.

The tenth resolution called for both the vocational and cultural training of young Blacks. This resolution proposed that neither type of training was superior to the other. However, conference officials demanded that young Blacks be afforded a holistic education to provide them with the skills needed to gain intellectual as well as vocational employment.

The 1910 study is noteworthy because it debunked the commonly held notion, largely promoted by Booker T. Washington and his support of vocational education, that Black Americans did not benefit from a liberal arts college education through the procurement of jobs. The data presented in this investigation indicated that not only did Black American college graduates increase their employment opportunities, they also increased their political and social capital.

Atlanta University Publication #16, 1911
"The Common School and the Negro American"
Edited by W. E. B. Du Bois and Augustus Granville Dill

The 1911 investigation, conference and publication addressed the status of Black common schools and were an extension of the 1901 investigation,

"The Negro Common School." The methods of data collection for this investigation included reviews of annual reports of the United States Commissioner of Education, state school reports, reports from various city school superintendents and reports from teachers and citizens in various southern communities.

Data from the United States Bureau of Education, together with reports from the years 1896, 1901 and 1902, were used to obtain demographic and economic information concerning public education and Black Americans. Data from these sources revealed the number of students and the amount of funding allotted for various schools committed to educating Black students.

State school reports were received from 17 mostly southern and Atlantic coast states and the District of Columbia. The data from these sources provided information concerning the number of students enrolled in school, the salaries of Black and White teachers, the total number of Black and White teachers, attendance of students, federal and state appropriations and illiteracy rates.

School superintendents in various states were mailed questionnaires requesting information concerning their location, the number of school buildings for Blacks in their district, the seating capacity of schools, numbers of Black students, numbers of Black teachers, institutions where teachers were educated, work habits of teachers, strengths and weaknesses of Black teachers, salaries and opinions on the work of Black schools. Replies were received from 124 superintendents representing 15 states.

School teachers and various citizens throughout the South were mailed questionnaires soliciting data concerning their location, numbers of White and Black schools in the area, length of school term for Black and White schools, numbers of Black and White teachers, amount of money spent on Black and White schools, school facilities and the general condition of Black schools in their area. The number of reports received from school teachers and various citizens was not identified.

This study, similar to previous ones, carried a disclaimer concerning the limitation of the data collected. The executive committee proclaimed:

> The object of these studies is primarily scientific—a careful research for truth; conducted thoroly (*sic*), broadly and honestly as the material resources and mental equipment at command will allow. It must be remembered that mathematical accuracy in these studies is impossible; the sources of information are of varying degrees of accuracy and the pictures are woefully incomplete. There is necessarily much repetition in the successive studies, and some contradiction of previous reports by later ones as new material comes to hand. (Du Bois and Dill 1911: 5)

Despite these limitations, the executive committee resolutely asserted that, "All we can claim is that the work is as thoro (*sic*) as circumstances permit and that with all its obvious limitations it is well worth the doing" (ibid.: 5). The resolutions below are presented in light of the limitations cited above.

The first resolution noted a reduction in the amount of money allotted to finance Black schools over the past few years. Data gathered for this study indicated how, for example, Houston County in Georgia educated 3,165 African American students and 1,044 White students, yet appropriated state funds for their education to the amounts of $4,509 and $10,678, respectively. This disparity in funding for Black students, as disheartening as the data appear, was actually an increase over what had been offered to Blacks over the previous ten years.

The second resolution reported that the wages of Black teachers were lower than those of their White counterparts. In North Carolina "the colored teachers were paid $224,800 in 1907 and $221,800 in 1908; during the same time the amount paid white teachers in the rural districts was increased by $50,000" (ibid.: 117). Additionally, it was argued by Atlanta University officials that many school districts in the American South preferred to employ poorly trained teachers than better qualified teachers in order to maintain low teacher salaries.

The third resolution charged that many superintendents neglected to properly supervise their Black schools. This neglect led to inferior buildings, poor educational resources and low salaries for Black teachers. A representative example of the neglect of Black schools was noted by Mr. W. K. Tate, state supervisor of elementary rural schools of South Carolina. Mr. Tate said:

> It has been my observation that the Negro schools of South Carolina are for the most part without supervision of any kind. Frequently the county superintendent does not know where they are located and sometimes the district board can not tell where the Negro school is taught. (ibid.: 103)

These comments indicate a gross neglect of South Carolina schools in particular and the prevailing apathy concerning Black schools throughout the South.

The fourth resolution indicated that few schools had been established for Black youth and that the current schools were in great need of repair. The executive committee reported that:

> It seems almost incredible that Atlanta with a Negro population of 51,902, Savannah with a Negro population of 33,246 and Augusta with a Negro

population of 18,344, should make no provision for the high school training of their black children. (ibid.: 127)

These data indicated the need for an educational program designed to serve the needs of the Black population.

The fifth resolution argued that Blacks were prevented from participating in the governance of their children's public schools. Atlanta University officials discovered that Black parents were denied input into the governance of their school systems via the electoral process because they were disenfranchised in their segregated communities. The eight methods of disfranchisement identified by the Atlanta Sociological Laboratory were:

1. Illiteracy: The voter must be able to read and write.
2. Property: The voter must own a certain amount of property.
3. Poll Tax: The voter must have paid his poll tax for the present year or a series of years.
4. Employment: The voter must have regular employment.
5. Army Service: Soldiers in the Civil War and certain other wars, or their descendants, may vote.
6. Reputation: Persons of good reputation who understand the duties of a citizen may vote.
7. 'Grandfather Clause' clause: Persons who could vote before the freedmen were enfranchised or descendants of such persons may vote.
8. Understanding Clause: Persons may vote who understand some selected clause of the Constitution and can explain it to the satisfaction of the registration officials. (ibid.: 115)

According to Atlanta University officials, disenfranchisement laws combined with the threat of physical violence by the Ku Klux Klan to make it virtually impossible for Blacks to exercise their right to participate in the democratic political process at this particular period in American history.

The 1911 study is noteworthy because, similar to previous studies, it provided scientific documentation of specific structural inequalities that made the exercise of the human and civil rights of Blacks through their participation in the American political process virtually impossible. Although full participation in the voting process would not be secured legislatively until the voting rights acts of the 1960s, efforts to limit the participation of Blacks were uncovered and documented here and could have been actively used to secure the rights guaranteed to Blacks via the American Constitution much sooner than during the modern Civil Rights movement.

Atlanta University Publication #17, 1912
"The Negro American Artisan"
Edited by W. E. B. Du Bois and Augustus Granville Dill

The 1912 investigation, conference and publication, "The Negro American Artisan," was an extension of the 1902 investigation and was revisited, in part, because of prevailing societal beliefs that "The Negro is lazy [and] Negroes have a childish ambition to do work for which they are not suited" (Du Bois and Dill 1912: 5). "This study is an attempt to get at facts underlying such widespread thot (*sic*) as this by making a study of the trained Negro laborer, his education, opportunity, wages and work ... The present study seeks to go over virtually the same ground [as the study conducted ten years prior]" (ibid.: 5). The methods of data collection included examinations of contemporary and classic studies of African life, ante-bellum American historical studies, local studies, reports from the United States Department of the Census, catalogs of African American colleges and universities, and questionnaires.

Studies of African life and ante-bellum American historical studies were used because "A study of the Negro American artisan quite naturally begins with the entrance of the Negro into American life" (ibid.: 24). The data gained from these sources identified the types of occupations and work habits of Africans immediately before and after their forced exodus to North America. United States Census data from the years 1850, 1860, 1870, 1880, 1890 and 1900, the catalog of Negro institutions and local studies from 41 states and the District of Columbia were used to identify the total number of Black workers in the United States and their specific occupations.

Questionnaires were mailed to four groups: interested citizens, heads of Black institutions, Black artisans and various labor unions across the nation. Data received from interested citizens focused on the number of Black laborers in specific communities, their specific trade, visible results of industrial training on African Americans and the success of Black tradesmen in the communities investigated. The heads of Black institutions provided data regarding specific occupations of graduates and their current location, difficulties they may have experienced while attempting to obtain work and the number of graduates currently teaching industrial education in schools. Data received from Black artisans included their wages, the location where their trade was learned, union affiliation, working relationship with whites, prejudice experienced in the workplace and the general condition of Black artisans. Information obtained from organizations such as the United Mine Workers of America, International Union of Pavers, Rammermen, Flaggers, Bridge and Stone Curb Setters, and Boot and Shoe Makers' Union produced data concerning the membership, or lack thereof, of Blacks, and the, if applicable, working relationship between Black and White employees. These methods of data collection combined to produce the resolutions presented at this conference.

The first resolution stated that Black skilled labor was gaining ground in both the North and South. This resolution was offered in response to census data and reports from artisans themselves indicating a growth in the number of skilled laborers garnering employment in both sections of the nation.

The second resolution asserted that the advancements of Black artisans were being accomplished despite the opposition and racial prejudice of Whites. For example, conference records indicate that:

> The opposition of white mechanics to Negro workmen which was evident in ante-bellum days became more intense after the emancipation of the slaves and in the competition which followed, the untutored, inexperienced black mechanic found himself outdistanced by his thriftier white competitor, sometimes by fair means, sometimes by foul. Without the protection, and with less of the patronage of his former master, the Negro artisan found himself being gradually supplanted by the white working man. (ibid.: 37)

Although faced with racial prejudice from working class Whites over competition for employment, Atlanta University officials asserted that Black artisans, as a group, were able to gain a foothold in many areas of skilled labor in the United States.

The third resolution encouraged Black laborers to embrace and support their fellow White laborers in a massive labor movement that could, ultimately, benefit them all. The 1912 publication reported that:

> The salvation of all laborers, white and black, lies in the great movement of social uplift known as the labor movement which has increased wages and decreased hours of labor for black as well as white. When the white laborer is educated to understand economic conditions he will outgrow his pitiable race prejudice and recognize that black men and white men in the labor world have a common cause. Let black men fight prejudice and exclusion in the labor world and fight it hard; but do not fight the labor movement. (ibid.: 7)

It is quite reasonable to assume that the executive committee recognized the exploitation of White as well as Black artisans and that this resolution was offered in the spirit of Karl Marx's notion of class consciousness. Realizing the immense economic and political power to be gained from an alliance of working class artisans, conference officials strongly supported a labor movement designed to unite Black and White workers.

The fourth resolution suggested that an emphasis be placed on liberal arts and technical training and asserted that it was fruitless to train people for jobless areas. The executive committee, similar to Du Bois's theory of the talented tenth, asserted that holistic education should be strongly encouraged because it equipped Blacks with the skills needed to survive in American society. An over emphasis on one type of training, which had been technical education to this point, would leave Blacks ill prepared to face the dilemmas of the ever growing American society that was becoming increasingly dependent upon mental rather than physical labor.

Atlanta University Publication #18, 1913
"Morals and Manners among Negro Americans"
Edited by W. E. B. Du Bois and Augustus Granville Dill

The 1913 investigation, conference and publication were titled, "Morals and Manners among Negro Americans." This topic was selected because "There is without a doubt a deep-seated feeling in the minds of many that the Negro problem is primarily a matter of morals and manners and that the real basis of color prejudice in America is the fact that the Negroes as a race are rude and thotless (*sic*) in manner and altogether quite hopeless in sexual morals, in regard for property rights and in reverence for truth" (Du Bois and Dill 1913: 5). The data collection methods used in this investigation consisted of the analysis, by a sociology class at Atlanta University, of United States Department of Census information, questionnaires and a local study.

1904 Department of Census data were examined by members of the sociology class at Atlanta University and their findings presented in a number of essays included in this publication. The research efforts of this class resulted in articles titled, 'Negro Americans in the United States,' 'The Negro American Farmer,' 'Marital Conditions among Negro Americans' and 'Religious Bodies among Negro Americans.'

Questionnaires were mailed to three groups African American churches, 'trustworthy persons' and 4,000 United States residents. Black churches in Atlanta were mailed questionnaires seeking information concerning the type of denomination, total membership, assets, expenditures expended for missions, educational activities, buildings and repairs, charitable work, care for old people, efforts at encouraging young people, other social services and the greatest challenge facing this institution. Replies were received from 55 of the 63 churches contacted. These data, also secured by students of a sociology class at Atlanta University, provided information concerning the morals and manners of some church going Blacks in Atlanta, Georgia.

Trustworthy persons were included in this investigation because Atlanta University officials believed this group "ought to know of the morals and manners of the Negro" (ibid.: 12). Data received from this group addressed manners, morals, cleanliness, honesty, home life, child rearing, caring of the elderly and a comparison of the present condition of Blacks with the conditions faced by the same group of people 10 to 20 years prior. This questionnaire was sent to 4,000 people and ten percent of the recipients, representing 30 states, replied.

The first resolution called for a strengthening of the home life of Black Americans even though conference data from numerous trustworthy persons and Black churches in Atlanta indicated an increase in the morality of Blacks over the past ten years. The second resolution advanced the proposition that there were two hindrances in the path of Black American advancement: the persistence of older habits due to slavery and poverty and racial prejudice. Conference officials suggested that habits learned during enslavement and the poverty stricken years of reconstruction were hindering the advancement of the race. The executive committee asserted:

> The environment of the American Negro has not been in the past and is not today conducive to the development of the highest morality. There is upon him still the heritage of two hundred and fifty years of slave regime. Slavery fosters certain virtues like humility and obedience, but these flourish at the terrible cost of lack of self respect, shiftlessness, tale bearing, slovenliness and sexual looseness. (ibid.: 16)

Ultimately, conference officials believed that only time would enable Blacks to cast off the grime of slavery and embrace the heightened morality of freedom. Additionally, this resolution included a statement indicating that racial prejudice continued to be a major problem and greatly impeded the moral advancement of the race. The third resolution acknowledged the awakening of the Black church to its duties and responsibility as a leading community organization and the fourth resolution commended the work of Black women's clubs in their efforts to better their various communities through social uplift. Neither of these resolutions was supported by tangible data.

The 1913 study signaled the end of Du Bois's 16-year association with the Atlanta University Study of the Negro Problems. Although he would return to Atlanta University in 1933 and attempt to revive the sociological laboratory that he led to prominence some years earlier, the 1913 study effectively marked the end of the first American school of sociology. Two monographs followed this investigation. However, the attempts to replicate Du Bois's standard of scientific excellence were not successful.

Atlanta University Publication #19, 1917
"Economic Cooperation among the Negroes of Georgia"
Edited by Thomas I. Brown

Because of America's involvement in World War I, the Atlanta University investigations were not conducted between 1913 and 1916. When the annual investigation was restarted, the 1917 study, conference and publication centered on 'Economic Cooperation among the Negroes of Georgia.' This study was a continuation of an investigation first explored in 1907.

> Ten years ago the Atlanta University Conference conducted an inquiry into the progress of 'Economic Co-Operation among Negro Americans.' That study, ably directed by Dr. W. E. B. Du Bois, aroused national attention and international interest. Following the arrangement by which the Atlanta University studies are repeated every ten years, the twenty-second annual Conference took up this year that study; but with this difference, that whereas the inquiry of 1907 was national in scope the present one has been confined to the state of Georgia. (Brown 1917: 9)

The methods of data collection included correspondences, a first-hand investigation by Asa H. Gordon (Atlanta University Class of 1917) and field work by members of the sociology class at Atlanta University.

Correspondences were made with 'business people and other responsible persons' regarding economic cooperation among Blacks in Georgia. Unlike previous Atlanta University investigations, the methods of data collection were not identified. Additionally, unlike most previous publications, data supporting the resolutions were not included in the final printing. A final difference between this and previous publications is that the data used in this investigation were compiled and presented in essay form by the editor, Thomas I. Brown.

Asa H. Gordon, a 1917 Atlanta University graduate, conducted first-hand investigations in "all cities and towns [in Georgia] having a population of ten thousand or more, and in some instances, for special reasons, places of less than ten thousand inhabitants" (ibid.: 9). Publication records indicate that "His mission was fruitful of good results; not only from the standpoint of actual information secured, but also from the point of view of his illuminating report on the conduct of Negro business throughout the state" (ibid.: 9). Gordon recorded an accurate number of Black businesses in the towns investigated and provided detailed descriptions of the conditions of the buildings and peculiarities of the businesses.

A final supplement to the data amassed by correspondence and Asa H. Gordon was fieldwork conducted by members of an Atlanta University sociology class. The city of Atlanta had recently experienced a disastrous fire that destroyed many Black businesses in the year preceding this investigation. Atlanta University students sought out every Black business in the area and amassed as much data as possible on the current state of those businesses. These data collection techniques formed the foundation for the resolutions offered by the executive committee.

The first resolution commended the progress made by Black businesspersons in Georgia. The second resolution criticized many Black businesses for lacking etiquette and not maintaining neat and clean establishments. The third resolution called for increased patronage of Black businesses. The final resolution commended interracial business cooperation. The 1917 study marked the first investigation conducted without the guidance or input of W. E. B. Du Bois and the difference in planning and quality was marked.

Atlanta University Publication #20, 1915
"Select Discussions of Race Problems"
Edited by J. A. Bingham

The 1915 Atlanta University publication consisted of a collection of essays on the race problem. Included in this volume were articles written by W. E. B. Du Bois, Felix von Luschan, Franklin P. Mall, R. S. Woodworth, W. I. Thomas, Franz Boas (two articles) and Alexander Francis Chamberlain. The publication of this monograph signaled the end of the first cycle of the Atlanta University Study of the Negro Problems and included nine resolutions that were based upon data collected during the first period of the Atlanta University Studies, 1896–1917.

The first resolution asserted that the death rate of Blacks had shown a downward tendency since 1896. The second resolution stated that Blacks were able to advance economically despite many hindrances placed in their path. The third resolution commended colleges and universities of this nation for improving the moral, social and economic condition of Blacks in America. The fourth resolution called for increased effort to educate children in the South because over 50 percent were not enrolled in high school. The fifth resolution suggested that the morals and ideals of Blacks were being raised with the assistance of common schools. The sixth resolution sought increased attention to, and the scientific study of, conditions that made criminals of Blacks. The seventh resolution posited that the monies expended upon the Atlanta University Conferences and reports were well spent. The eighth resolution asserted that "these social studies have furnished one of the most important contributions, in tested facts and scientific conclusions, toward a foundation for the advancement of the Negro in the United States"

(Bingham 1915: 9). Last, the ninth resolution called for the continuation of future Atlanta University studies and reports.

"I Insist On My Right to Think and Speak"

When the final publication of the Atlanta University Study of the Negro Problems was released in 1917, the first era of the Atlanta Sociological Laboratory effectively ended. The fruits of this research program included conferences that were held between 1896 and 1924, publications released between 1896 and 1917 and immense and varied contributions to the discipline. One can only wonder what impact this school would have had on the discipline had it continued under the direction of W. E. B. Du Bois. It was mentioned earlier that Du Bois left the faculty of Atlanta University in 1910, yet remained as director of the annual studies until 1914. What was not discussed was the cause of Du Bois's departure from the faculty in 1910 and the university altogether in 1914.

Most are familiar with the ideological sparring that occurred between Du Bois and Booker T. Washington at the turn of the century. At the heart of their intellectual disagreement was Washington's Atlanta Compromise speech, in which Du Bois believed that Washington, being the recognized pre-eminent Black American leader at that time, effectively traded away the civil rights of American Blacks in return for the favor and grace of mainstream White America. Stern in this belief, Du Bois engaged in aggressive attacks against Washington and those who supported his position. While Du Bois was engaged in his battles with Washington, he had no idea, at least initially, about how that sparring would negatively affect him and Atlanta University. Speaking about the intensity and implications of his intellectual disagreements with Washington, Du Bois (1968: 223–224) said:

> [T]here came a controversy between Booker T. Washington and myself, which became more personal and bitter than I had ever dreamed and which necessarily dragged in the university ... I did not at the time see the handwriting on the wall. I did not realize how strong the forces were back of [Booker T. Washington's] Tuskegee [University] and how they might interfere with my scientific study of the Negro.

Du Bois believed Washington's allies, possibly acting on the wishes of the Wizard of Tuskegee, were attempting to starve Atlanta University of funds needed to support the already inadequately funded institution and its sociological research endeavor. Du Bois offers as evidence a story of his experience with a Mr. Schiff, a well-known philanthropist who he believed could be of great assistance in his effort to obtain funding for "a high-class journal to circulate among the intelligent Negroes" (ibid.: 224). After writing a letter of inquiry, according to Du Bois:

> Mr. Schiff wrote back courteously, saying: 'Your plans to establish a high-class journal to circulate among the intelligent Negroes is in itself interesting, and on its face has my sympathy. But before I can decide whether I can become an advantage in carrying your plans into effect, I would wish to advise with men whose opinion in such a matter I consider of much value.' Nothing ever came of this, because, as I might have known, most of Mr. Schiff's friends were strong and sincere advocates of [Booker T. Washington and] Tuskegee. (ibid.: 224–225)

Although there exists no empirical evidence of Washington's interference in the procuring of philanthropic gifts by Atlanta University, it is without question that Du Bois believed Washington and his friends to have played a role, even if a minor one, in the school's difficulties in amassing funding. Additionally, it was not lost on Du Bois that the subject matter of the annual investigations and some of the findings that were critical of institutional American racism made the school and his attempts to garner funding difficult.

Once it became obvious to Du Bois that he was the biggest hindrance to the school receiving philanthropic gifts he made a selfless decision. In his 1913 letter of resignation from the faculty of Atlanta University Du Bois (ibid.: 229) wrote:

> I insist on my right to think and speak; but if that freedom is made an excuse for abuse of and denial of aid to Atlanta University, then with regret I shall withdraw from Atlanta University.

Reflecting on his departure from the faculty at Atlanta University in an unpublished 1940 speech at the First Congregational Church in Atlanta, Georgia, Du Bois ([1940] 1981: 4) lamented, "the final study of which I was directly connected was a study of Morals and Manners. I then left for work with the National Association for the Advancement of Colored People in New York and took up publication of the Crisis." Although he resigned from the faculty, Du Bois remained as director of the research program until 1914. After World War I began in 1914, the investigation, conference and publication were placed on hiatus for a number of years. The entire research effort officially ended when the final conference was hosted by the school in 1924. When the Atlanta University Study of the Negro Problems ended, many people, foremost among them Du Bois, mourned the loss of the influential sociological research center. For Du Bois, the most significant impact of the defunct program of sociological research on the social, economic and physical condition of Blacks in America is the fact that expertise in this area of inquiry was transferred from the all-Black institution to PWIs like the University of North Carolina and the University of Chicago. Directly addressing this notion, Du Bois (ibid.: 5) said, "I have always regretted that the work had to stop when it did and that a period of nearly twenty years went by when leadership in the social study of the Negro passed from the Negro's own hands here in Atlanta to the hands of white people in North Carolina and many Northern institutions."

The Atlanta Sociological Laboratory remained dormant until a visionary university leader reached out to its primary architect and asked him to restart the research program. In 1933, Atlanta University President John Hope asked Du Bois to return to the school to revive the annual investigation, conference and publication. The revived Atlanta University Study of the Negro Problems was renamed Phylon Institute. According to Du Bois (1940: 4):

> This effort of ours is, in a sense, a revival of the old Atlanta University Publications issued between 1897 and 1914. Those publications formed the first scientific basis for factual study of the condition and relations of one racial group in the United States, and was the beginning in America of applied Sociology and Anthropology to group problems. This pioneer work has been supplemented widely since 1914 by institutions like Fisk University and the University of North Carolina, and by individual students like [E. Franklin Frazier, Charles S. Johnson and Abram Harris].

Once again, garnering philanthropic support equal to that of a University of Chicago type institution proved difficult. However, Du Bois did garner some financial support from the Carnegie Foundation to support publications and conferences in 1941, 1943 and 1944. Additionally, a third report was published in 1947. While Du Bois was not on pace to rebuild the research program that he had so deftly spearheaded in the early twentieth century, at a minimum, the land grant institutions that formed the foundation of the Phylon Institute were dedicated to engaging in research centered on investigating and improving the condition of Blacks in America. Unfortunately, before Du Bois ([1960] 1981: 36) could fully develop his second era of Atlanta University studies, "Without notice to me of any kind, I was retired from my professorship and headship of the department of sociology at Atlanta University." According to Dorothy C. Yancy (1978), Atlanta University had a long standing retirement age policy for faculty. When Du Bois returned to Atlanta University in 1933 he was already 65 years of age. Du Bois did not expect the age policy to be employed against him, given his age upon return and his continued scholarly productivity. Unfortunately for Du Bois, President Hope died a few years after facilitating his return to the university.

Many years after President Hope's death, "[Atlanta University] President Rufus Clement recommended Du Bois's retirement to the Board of Trustees and the Board agreed" (ibid.: 64). Certain that the decision to retire him from service at Atlanta University was rooted in institutional politics, Du Bois ([1960] 1981: 37) lamented:

> My sudden retirement then savored of a deliberate plot, although this cannot be proven. The retirement age at Atlanta University was sixty-five. But I was sixty-five when President Hope called me to the University. Nothing was said between us about the conditions of eventual retirement – due to my usual neglect of financial considerations and because my good health gave me no thought of stopping my work at any near time. Hope must have mentioned the matter to Florence Reed, treasurer, but they reached no decision that I knew of.

Du Bois believed that President Clement and School Treasurer Reed conspired to have him retired for separate reasons.

> I opposed Miss Reed's election to succeed Hope; and the new plan gained me wide acclaim. Even the General Education Board which handled Rockefeller Funds favored my plan. President Clement while supporting the plan was not enthusiastic. As a new young unknown president, perhaps, he saw my reputation overshadowing him. Letters came to me; visitors asked for me and no doubt Miss reed encouraged his jealousy. I was conscious that this might occur and tried to be careful. (ibid.: 37)

Du Bois's belief that a plot rooted in retribution and jealousy was further engrained by events at the meeting that led up to his retirement. As he indicated:

> Neither Miss Reed nor President Clement said a word to me about retirement; but at a meeting of the Board of Trustees, in 1944, Miss Reed proposed that I be retired. President Clement seconded the motion and apparently with little or no objection the Board passed the vote. Presumably most of the members assumed that the matter had been discussed with me and had my agreement. No pension was mentioned. (ibid.: 38)

In a rather unceremonious fashion, the short lived second era of the Atlanta Sociological Laboratory ended upon Du Bois's forced retirement from Atlanta

University in 1944. Although Du Bois no longer had an institutional home for his annual investigation and resultant publication:

> [T]here were some earnest attempts to carry the proposed program on. [The Phylon Institute] was transferred to Howard University, with E. Franklin Frazier in charge. An excellent conference was held in 1945. But Frazier was not given funds for continuing the project and the Land Grant Colleges gradually ceased to cooperate. The whole scheme died within a year or two. It has never been revived. (ibid.: 39)

Between 1896 and 1924, social scientists at Atlanta University conducted sociological research on the social, economic and physical condition of Blacks in America at a time when objective studies on these topics were few and far between. The researchers associated with this endeavor were singularly focused on studying and, if possible, improving the condition of Blacks in America. They were not concerned with the groundbreaking nature of their work. However, during the course of conducting research on the conditions of Blacks in America, the Du Bois-led Atlanta Sociological Laboratory did amass a number of substantive contributions to sociology and the social sciences. What follows in the next chapter is a presentation of this school's tremendous, yet still overlooked contributions to the discipline of sociology.

Chapter 3

The Contributions of the Atlanta Sociological Laboratory to the Discipline

In the preceding chapters I outlined the origin of Atlanta University, the establishment of the Atlanta University Study of the Negro Problems and W. E. B. Du Bois's role in directing the school of sociology, and gave a detailed accounting of the methods of data collection, major findings and resolutions of each study conducted between 1896 and 1917. Over the nearly 30-year life span of the Atlanta University studies and conferences, Du Bois and the members of his sociological laboratory engaged in research and practices that resulted in substantive contributions to the discipline. Despite not benefitting from the philanthropic largesse of faithful supporters of higher education like the Rockefeller and Carnegie families, the poorly funded all-Black institution in the deep American South managed to conduct one of the first studies debunking scientific racism theories concerning Blacks, become the first American sociological unit to institutionalize the acknowledgement of the limitations of one's research, become the first American sociological unit to institutionalize use of the insider researcher, become the first American sociological unit to institutionalize method triangulation and established the first American school of sociology. Each of these achievements is discussed below.

Challenging Theories of Scientific Racism

Scientific racism dates back to the Ancient Greeks, when one's classification as free or slave was grounded in a class, rather than a race position and was accompanied with specific assumptions about one's biological and intellectual capabilities. Greek philosophers and leading thinkers of their respective eras, Plato and Aristotle, are said to have "arbitrarily assigned slaves of all races a lesser status within the human family. They speculated that slaves were inherently inferior and less intelligent" (Byrd and Clayton 2001: 175). As Europeans began to increase their colonialist and imperialist desires for control over world resources, rationalization of the domination of African lands shifted from the class based model promoted by Plato and Aristotle to one rooted squarely in skin color and supported by laypersons because of the supposed intellectual inferiority and biological deficits of Blacks vis-à-vis Whites. It was not long before trained scientists, in the fields of both social science and medicine, adopted a perspective now referred to as *scientific racism* to legitimate within the academic community a scientific theoretical frame to explain the inferiority of Blacks and, by extension, validate the exploitation of a continent filled with vast resources and the enslavement of its *childlike* peoples. "Thus," according to Clayton (ibid.: 176), "succeeding generations of internationally respected western natural scientists and physicians provided mounting 'evidence' that supported the Western European cultural assumptions of white superiority and black biologic and intellectual inferiority." By the time slavery reached its climax in the United States the *scientific* data produced by the medical and social science communities were conclusive in their assessments of the biological and intellectual acuity, or lack thereof, of Blacks vis-à-vis Whites. Blacks were conclusively and *scientifically* found to be lesser and inferior beings. So entrenched was this belief that American medical professionals had developed categories of diseases that only affected Blacks. For example, the *disease* that caused Blacks to escape their masters during enslavement was known as drapetomania and the *disease* that accounted for the dark color, enlarged lips, flat nose and wooly hair of Blacks was called chronic leprosy. It was within this national, international and sociological milieu that Du Bois and the men and women of Atlanta University, in 1906, conducted a study that produced results challenging the long held notion of the biological inferiority of Blacks.

I will not review the study in full here since that task was performed in Chapter 2. However, I will emphasize here that the fourth resolution of the 1906 study indicated that no evidence was found to support the existing literature's promotion of the physical inferiority of Blacks vis-à-vis Whites. W. Montague Cobb, who in 1932 became the first African American to earn the Ph.D. in anthropology in the United States and the only one to accomplish that task until after the Korean war some 20 years later, commented on the significance of the 1906 *Health and Physique of the Negro American* study and its potential usefulness in debunking the hegemonic scientific racism theories of the early twentieth century. Cobb argued that Du Bois set the stage for the eradication of scientific racism theories. Unfortunately, neither the medical nor social science communities were yet prepared to embrace, support and promote such a notion. Despite the academic community's collective disregard of the work produced at Atlanta University in 1906, there is agreement in the exiting literature that the era of scientific racism effectively ended after World War II when the atrocities committed against Jews were uncovered.

After World War II the United Nations, in its capacity as the guiding international institution engaged in the promotion of global equality, actively advanced the position that all world citizens were equal (biologically, intellectually and in all other manners) regardless of race, gender, religion, etc. The United Nations was so committed to dispelling theories of scientific racism that a subcommittee of the organization was asked "to consider the desirability of initiating and recommending the general adoption of a programme of disseminating scientific facts, designed to remove what is generally known as racial prejudice" (Comas 1961: 304). Shortly thereafter, educational campaigns were initiated and scientific studies debunking scientific racism released. In the information disseminated to "remove racial prejudice", one category was noteworthy because the findings seemingly replicated conclusions reached by Du Bois 50 years earlier. In the category of physical characteristics a question was raised.

> Is it possible, biologically speaking, to certify a group to be superior or inferior by such criteria as its physical characteristics? [Around 1930] Vallois categorically refuted this position, and demonstrated convincingly that the Negro was not physically inferior to the White. (ibid.: 307)

That the United Nations arrived at this conclusion utilizing a study conducted in the 1930s is noteworthy inasmuch as the same argument was presented by Du Bois and his Atlanta University research team in 1906 but, obviously, was not taken seriously by the mainstream scientific community.

Research Methods

Research on the origin, history and early practitioners of data collection methods in sociology is limited. It was not until 1996 that Jennifer Platt (1996: i) authored "the first book on the general history of US sociological research methods." Given the incompleteness of the existing literature, Platt warned readers not to expect a thorough examination on this topic dating back to the discipline's mid-nineteenth-century American origins. *A History of Sociological Research Methods in America, 1920–1960*, according to Platt (ibid.: 4), "does not attempt to fill the gaps with a complete narrative history (on the development of research methods in the United States), but draws on narrative materials in relation to key thematic issues." Although she does not offer a complete history of research methods in the United States, Platt does provide a foundation upon which my claims concerning the methodological contributions of the Du Bois-led Atlanta Sociological Laboratory are established. Making the argument for the chosen time period of her project, Platt (ibid.: 2) writes, "[t]he book takes as its remit the period in American sociology from around 1920, when university sociologists started to carry out empirical work and to write about research methods, until around 1960." While it may be true that mainstream White sociologists began taking seriously the issue of research methods in their writings circa 1920, Du Bois and his research team had been engaged in empirical research and writing on their data collection methods since the late 1890s. While this time period does not predate the establishment of the University of Chicago's department of sociology, it certainly predates the period of Atlanta University's chief rival and most decorated American school of sociology—the Robert Park and Ernest Burgess-led Chicago School of Sociology.

The Chicago School of Sociology is the moniker bestowed on social scientists engaged in sociological work at the University of Chicago circa 1915–1930. Historically recognized as comprising the first American school of sociology, a notion that is debunked later in this chapter, the Chicago School is noted for its contributions to the discipline in a number of areas including, but not limited to, urban sociology and ethnography. One area for which it is not recognized is research methods. While it is demonstrable that the Atlanta Sociological Laboratory took very seriously the relationship between data collection methods and research conclusions in the late 1890s, Platt argues that neither the Chicago School nor the contemporary mainstream White American sociological enterprise embraced this same notion. In fact, "The sense that the weight of empirical conclusions rested on the merit of the methods by which they had been reached was not yet clearly established in the 1920s, and even at the University of Chicago, where much important research was done, the publications based on it were often extremely vague about the status and origins of their data" (ibid.: 34).

Martyn Hammersley (1989: 86), providing additional support for Platt's argument on the Chicagoans early lack of methodological sophistication or awareness, writes, "for the most part within [the] Chicago [School] ... limited attention seems to have been given to methodology." Hammersley (ibid.: 83) continues, "What is also surprising about the Chicago research is [the] relative absence of methodological discussion about the use of different kinds of data and the problems of interpreting them. Many types of data are presented in the same form as 'documents.'" Hammersley (ibid.: 84) completes his critique by asserting:

> It is ironic, then, that in general the Chicagoans provide little information about how their research was carried out or about the data used. Zorbaugh gives virtually no information. Anderson simply lists documents, giving a brief description of each. Cressey wrote an informative article about his research methods, but it was not published at the time.

Platt (1987: 3) provides a concluding statement on the methodological practices of early Chicago sociologists when she states:

[W]hen we look at the Chicago studies it seems clear that … it was regarded as relatively unimportant who obtained the material, whether it was originally oral or written, and whether it reported scientific incidents or generalizations. What seems to have been taken as of overriding significance is that the documents have 'objective existence' in written form.

While it is clear that the Chicago School and White American sociological enterprise paid little attention to the importance of methodological clarity in its research projects prior to the 1920s, it is equally clear that methodological clarity and sophistication were important components of the Atlanta University Study on the Negro Problems both prior to and during Du Bois's tenure. It is for the reasons cited above, and discussed in detail below, that the Atlanta Sociological Laboratory should be recognized as being the first American sociological unit to institutionalize the public acknowledgement of the limitations of one's research, the first American sociological unit to institutionalize use of the insider researcher and the first American sociological unit to institutionalize method triangulation or mixed method data collection.

Acknowledgement of the Limitations of the Research

In Chapter 2 the methods of data collection are detailed for every study conducted between 1896 and 1917. During that period the school, when applicable, openly admitted its methodological failings. What follows are a few examples of the school's acknowledged methodological flaws. At the first Atlanta University conference, in 1896, President Bumstead, as presented in Chapter 2, cited the limitations of that year's study and committed the school to gathering the most accurate and scientific data possible on the social, economic and physical condition of Blacks in America, via the efforts of the most skilled social scientist they could find to lead their research endeavor. The school's commitment to this idea was continued by Du Bois upon his arrival a few years later. The third Atlanta University publication, the first led by Du Bois, included an acknowledgment of its limitations in the same manner as President Bumstead some years earlier. Du Bois (1898: 42) acknowledged that the data presented "include many of the more important enterprises, but not all … of them. It gives a rough, incomplete, and yet fairly characteristic picture of what the freedmen's sons are doing to better their social condition." The 1904 publication also included an acknowledgement of that study's limitations. It was acknowledged that "these data are less complete than in the case of our previous studies and few conclusions can be drawn until further facts and figures are available. The forthcoming government report on crime will undoubtedly be of great aid in further study" (Du Bois 1904: v). A final example comes from the 1908 study where it was noted that no generalizations to the larger

Black population could be drawn because of the inadequate representation of subjects. Du Bois (1908: 9–10) suggested that the findings:

> Do not, however, represent properly the proportion of different types among the masses of Negroes. Most of the families studied belong to the upper half of the Black population. Finally, to repeat, this study is but a sketch with no pretense toward attempting to exhaust a fruitful subject. The main cause of its limitation is lack of material.

There is no evidence of an institutionalized program of publicly acknowledging the limitations of one's sociological research prior to the Du Bois-led Atlanta Sociological Laboratory. Accordingly, this school should be acknowledged properly in the sociological literature as the architects of this technique. Notwithstanding this school's contributions in this area, its methodological sophistication extended beyond the acknowledgement of the limitations of its research. It also included the first institutionalized program of insider researchers.

Insider Researchers

A second methodological contribution of the Atlanta Sociological Laboratory is the institutionalization of the insider researcher. When the first Atlanta University study was launched in 1895 the Thirteenth Amendment to the United States Constitution ending the enslavement of Blacks in America had only been the law of the land for 30 years. Despite passage of the Thirteenth Amendment shadow forms of slavery like sharecropping and the convict lease system effectively continued the American tradition of bonded servitude or incarceration of Blacks. Sharecropping was a process whereby Blacks were kept in a perpetual state of indebtedness and poverty as a result of their employment on farms once called plantations. Sharecroppers were forced to purchase from the land owner all of the supplies needed to farm the land allotted to them. Additionally, sharecroppers were charged a fee for the land used. At the end of the harvest season sharecroppers were expected to pay their bill by amassing a certain poundage of crops. Because Blacks had few or no rights that Whites were bound to respect or that were legally protected, they were vulnerable to unscrupulous property owners. For example, it could be agreed between the parties that the sharecropper would need to produce 100 pounds of cotton at the end of the year to satisfy his bill. If at the end of the harvest season the sharecropper accumulated the necessary poundage and believed his obligation was met, they remained vulnerable to devious property owners who often reported to the sharecropper that, according to their scale, they did not meet their poundage obligation. Legal recourse for Blacks at this time was restricted, if it existed at all. Property owners, understanding the control they had over the lives of their employees, would then advance the sharecroppers a credit for the next year's supplies. This meant that the sharecropper would carry a debt from the previous year and add onto that the forthcoming debt for the next season. Options for Blacks within this system were limited. If a sharecropper attempted to leave the farm without paying the monies owed, fairly or unfairly, he could be arrested, placed into prison and become a part of the convict lease system.

Convict leasing was a second *de facto* form of slavery that existed after passage of the Thirteenth Amendment to the United States Constitution. Convict leasing was a process whereby *de facto* and *de jure* laws governing the lives of Blacks were established and practiced, principally in the American South. Black Codes are an example of the *de facto* laws that governed the actions and opportunities available to Blacks. Examples of Black Codes include the notion that Blacks were not to look a White person directly in the eye and the requirement that Blacks step off the sidewalk on approaching a White person, so as to allow the White person to continue in his or her path uninhibitedly. *De jure* laws included regulations such as maintaining employment at all times and not being part of a public gathering of more than two Blacks on a street corner at any time. The violation of either of these types of laws could result, at worst, in the loss of one's life and, at best, a beating or imprisonment. Once imprisoned a person's labor was often leased to private companies offering the highest bid on the services of the inmate. Theoretically, the inmate could serve the duration of his or her term, or life, as the literal slave of a private entity. Du Bois (1904: 2 and 4) wrote:

> Mr. Wines, the American criminologist, has said, 'A modified form of slavery survives wherever prison labor is sold to private persons for their pecuniary profit' ... Throughout the South laws were immediately passed authorizing public officials to lease the labor of convicts to the highest bidder. The lessee then took charge of the convicts—worked them as he wished under the normal control of the state. Thus a new slavery and slave-trade was established.

Atlanta University officials took very seriously the fact that abuses by Whites via sharecropping, the convict lease system and general domestic terrorism via the Ku Klux Klan, rendered most Blacks extremely hesitant about either cooperating with the investigative efforts of even the most upstanding White researcher or providing accurate data to someone they could not say with any level of confidence would not use the information gathered in an injurious fashion. Guided by this reality, the race of persons selected to be researchers for the annual investigations became vitally important and the need for *insiders* was stressed. The lack of trust in White researchers coalesced with a dearth of trained Black social scientists and a supply of Atlanta University graduates who could serve as researchers to form the first institutionalized program of insider researchers.

Because of the paucity of trained Black social scientists during this era, school officials often used citizen researchers to assist with data collection. These insider citizen researchers were often graduates or students of Atlanta University, students from other predominantly Black institutions and, on occasion, Black students from predominately White institutions. The benefit of utilizing insider citizen researchers was acknowledged in the inaugural 1896 Atlanta University publication by President Bumstead when he stated:

> Nearly all of the graduates of Atlanta University are living and working in the cities and larger towns of the South. This fact is very suggestive, for the problems of Negro city life must be settled largely by Negroes themselves, and the body of our alumni are in some respects specifically fitted for this task. (Atlanta University 1896: 6)

Commenting on the training received at one of the highest ranking colleges or universities in the United States at the time, President Bumstead continued:

> Not only are they familiar with the conditions of life in cities, but they have acquired, in their training in this institution, some degree of accurate observation and careful reflection, some acquaintance with high standards of living, some familiarity with measures of reform and of social and economic improvement that are indispensable for dealing with such matters. (ibid.: 6)

Although the use of insider citizen researchers was practiced prior to his arrival, Du Bois agreed with the idea that these bodies of semi-trained members of his sociological laboratory were essential to the annual investigations. In fact, the repeated use of the same body of data collectors would eventually result in a well-trained and valuable army of researchers. Du Bois (1899: 4) believed that "by calling on the same persons [as researchers] year after year, a body of experienced correspondents had been gradually formed, numbering ... about fifty." An example of the significance of employing insider citizen researchers on Atlanta University investigations can be found in the 1897 study. Moreover, this excerpt speaks directly of the utility of using Black insider researchers to the exclusion of White researchers:

> All the data gathered by this body of trained colored leaders, are believed to be, perhaps, more than usually accurate because of the investigators' knowledge of the character, habits, and prejudices of the people, and because of the fact that they were not hindered by the suspicions which confront the white investigator,

and which seriously affect the accuracy of the answers to his questions. (Atlanta University 1897: 5)

Again, while the use of non-university trained researchers was not ideal, its utilization was utilitarian given the lack of trained Black social scientists during the era and the suspicion that Blacks had of White researchers. Despite these facts, there is no evidence in the existing literature that suggests that this methodological technique was institutionalized at any program of sociology in the United States prior to that of the Atlanta Sociological Laboratory.

Method Triangulation (Mixed Methods)

Although Platt suggests that method triangulation did not emerge in the discipline until the middle of the twentieth century, Chapter 2 offers evidence of an institutionalized program of triangulation, or mixed method data collection, as early as 1897. Bruce L. Berg offers an understanding of triangulation, or mixed methods, that is used to frame the data collection techniques of the Atlanta Sociological Laboratory. According to Berg (2004: 5):

> For many researchers, triangulation is restricted to the use of multiple data gathering techniques (usually three) to investigate the same phenomenon. This is interpreted as a means of mutual confirmation of measures and validation of findings ... Fielding and Fielding (1986: p. 31) ... suggest that the important feature of triangulation is not the simple combination of different kinds of data but the attempt to relate them so as to counteract threats to validity in each.

Since the methods of data collection are detailed in full in Chapter 2, I will not subject the reader to a complete rehashing of that information. However, using Berg and Fielding and Fielding's understandings as the guide, examples of the earliest mixed methods employed by the school and its most detailed are highlighted.

The earliest example of triangulation is found in the 1897 Atlanta University study, "Social and Physical Condition of Negroes in Cities." The research question guiding this investigation was simply, "what is the social and physical condition of Blacks in American cities?" The data collection techniques included questionnaires received from more than 1,000 families, the examination of 15 years of health reports from multiple cities across America, reports collected from citizen researchers from more than 18 cities and data collected from more than 100 families that migrated from North Carolina to Massachusetts. The most detailed example of triangulation is the 1902 Atlanta University study, "The Negro Artisan." The research question guiding this study was, "what is the current condition of Black artisans in the United States?" The methods of data collection included questionnaires sent to more than 500 American workers and a separate and distinctly different questionnaire sent to more than 200 American employers to ensure validity, questionnaires to every American trade union, questionnaires received from more than 200 'central labor bodies,' reports from 32 states via citizen researchers, responses from industrial schools across the nation and information gathered by a newspaper in Chattanooga, Tennessee on the topic. The methods of data collection employed by the *Chattanooga Tradesman* included distinct sets of questionnaires delivered to the employers of Black artisans, southern educators and public school children. Without question the 1902 Atlanta University study represented the school's seminal methodological accomplishment and a blueprint for sociological inquiry in the United States.

The First American School of Sociology

While the contributions identified heretofore are significant in their own right, perhaps the most impressive accomplishment of the Atlanta Sociological Laboratory is its establishment of the first American school of sociology. There are varying understandings of what comprises a school in the sociological literature. The definition of school used here captures the essence of how the term has been used historically in the discipline. I agree with Bulmer (1985: 61) when he proposes that:

> A 'school' in the social sciences may be thought of as akin to the term used in art history to designate a group of contemporaries sharing a certain style, technique or set of symbolic expressions, and having at some point or other in time or space a high degree of interaction.

Bulmer (ibid.: 61) expands on the application of the term in the social sciences when he argues that:

> Schools of social science, particularly those committed to systematic empirical inquiry, are sufficiently unusual to merit some consideration. Most university departments of sociology are an assemblage of more or less independent scholars, pursuing diverse interests either individually or in small groups. They cooperate for purposes of teaching and administration, but in research go their own way. Any suggestion that there should be an integrated research program across a department, or that individuals should orient their research to certain central themes, ideas or problems, would be regarded by most academic sociologists as anathema.

While schools of social science, according to Bulmer, are uncommon, they are not unprecedented. In addition to providing a definition of the term, Bulmer outlines the criteria that must be met for a unit to be labeled a school. Although multiple conceptions of what constitutes a school exist in the literature, by far, Bulmer's offering is the most detailed and is used here to ascertain whether or not the W. E. B. Du Bois-led Atlanta Sociological Laboratory constituted a school. If yes, then Atlanta University, not the University of Chicago, is the location of the first American school of sociology. Bulmer's criteria for a school are:

> There must be a central figure around whom the department is organized. A school must exist in a university setting and have direct contact with a student population. There must be interaction between those who work at the university and the general community in which the university is located. A school must have, as its key figure, someone with a dominating personality. The leader of a school must possess an intellectual vision and have a missionary drive. There must be intellectual exchanges between colleagues and graduate students (e.g., the existence of seminars) and the school must have an outlet for the publication of scholarship written by members of the school. A school must have an adequate infrastructure (e.g., advances in research methods, institutional links and strong philanthropic support). A school cannot last beyond the generation of its central figure. A school must be open to ideas and influences beyond its home discipline.

In his article Bulmer (1985) concludes that the second generation of University of Chicago sociologists, led by Robert Park and Ernest Burgess, comprised the first American school of sociology circa 1915–1935. Bulmer (1984: xv) extends this praise because they met the criteria cited above and because he believes "the Chicago school represented the first successful American program of collective social research." Heretofore these arguments have been accepted and advanced by nearly every sociologist trained in the United States. However, it is proposed here that, using the definition of and criteria for a school as offered by Bulmer, the Atlanta Sociological Laboratory, not the Chicago School of Sociology, should henceforth be recognized as having established the first school of sociology and the first successful program of collective research in the United States.

Atlanta University: The First American School of Sociology

Bulmer's first criterion for a school is that it be organized around a central figure. Although George G. Bradford was the director of the first two Atlanta

University studies, W. E. B. Du Bois was the central figure around whom the Atlanta Sociological Laboratory was organized. Upon his arrival at Atlanta University in 1897, he implemented his plan of social science inquiry that continued until the cessation of the publications in 1917 and the conference in 1924. Du Bois's tenure as a member of the faculty at Atlanta University lasted from 1897 to 1910. After his 1910 resignation he continued to serve as director of the studies with the assistance of a former student.

> After the retirement of Du Bois in 1910 to become editor of the Crisis and director of publicity in the newly organized National Association for the Advancement of Colored People, his successor as professor of sociology was Augustus G. Dill, an Atlanta University graduate of the class of 1906, of Harvard in 1908, and who also continued the work of the conferences. Mr. Dill had, however, the benefit of a certain measure of assistance from Dr. Du Bois, whose name still appeared in the catalogue as director of the conference. (Adams 1930: 93–94)

Despite Adams's suggestion that Du Bois provided assistance to Dill for the investigations, there is little evidence to support the notion that Du Bois's role in identifying the research question guiding the studies, developing the methods of data collection or compiling the findings in the annual publication was less pronounced than in the years that he served singularly as the director of the research program.

The second criterion for a school mandates that it exist within a university setting and has direct contact with a student population. Moreover, this criterion includes an emphasis on the physical location of the university and "the training [of] graduates in research [rather than] undergraduate teaching that was common in universities in the English speaking world" (Bulmer 1985: 64). That Atlanta, Georgia was the ideal location for a program of research on the study of Blacks at the turn of the twentieth century was not lost on Du Bois ([1903] 1978: 62–63) as he noted that:

> Atlanta University is situated within a few miles of the geographical center of the Negro population of the nation, and is, therefore, near the centre of that congeries of human problems which cluster round the black American. This institution, which forms in itself a 'Negro problem,' and which prepares students whose lives must of necessity be further factors in this same problem, cannot logically escape the study and teaching of some things connected with that mass of social questions.

United States census data support Du Bois's assertion that Atlanta was the epicenter of the Black population, as Georgia had the highest total number (the only state to have more than one million Blacks) and percentage (only one of two states with double digits) of Blacks of any state according to the 1900 census (Wilcox 1904). Undoubtedly, Atlanta's location in the heart of the Black Belt made it an ideal location for a program of research on the social, economic and physical condition of urban and rural Blacks in the United States.

Another condition of this criterion is that the school has direct contact with a student population. Atlanta University, having established one of the earliest departments of sociology in the United States, had an extensive program of both undergraduate and graduate training for its students. Du Bois ([1903] 1978: 62–63) explained the opportunities available for undergraduate students at Atlanta University thus:

> We have arranged, therefore, what amounts to about two years of sociological work for the junior and senior college students … Our main object in the undergraduate work, however, is human training and not the collection of material, and in this we have been fairly successful. The classes are enthusiastic and of average intelligence, and the knowledge of life and of the meaning of life in the modern world is certainly much greater among these students than it would be without such a course of study.

While the emphasis on undergraduate training centered on teaching students how to understand the world through a sociological lens, Atlanta University officials understood the importance and necessity of instruction in graduate research with an applied focus. Du Bois offers insight into the school's graduate program in stating:

> Our postgraduate work in sociology was inaugurated with the thought that a university is primarily a seat of learning, and that Atlanta University, being in the midst of the Negro problems, ought to become a centre of such a systematic and thoroughgoing study of those problems as would gradually raise many of the questions above the realm of opinion and guess into scientific knowledge. (ibid.: 62–63)

The result was a graduate program in sociology that occasionally resulted in publishable material directed at improving the condition of Blacks in America.

> [W]e carry on in our conferences postgraduate work in original work … Sometimes [the original work conducted by undergraduates and postgraduates for the Atlanta University studies] are of real scientific value: the class of '99 furnished local studies, which, after some rearrangement, were published in No. 22 of the Bulletin of the United States Department of Labor; the work of another class was used in a series of articles on the housing of the Negro in the

Southern Workman, and a great deal of the work of other classes has been used in the reports of the Atlanta Conferences. (ibid.: 62–63)

The third criterion for a school dictates that there must be interaction between those who work at the university and the general community in which the university is located. Part of the interaction between the school and community has been described previously via the participation of citizens as researchers and data collectors for the yearly studies. Additional examples of interactions with the community are found in the activities of Du Bois. Evidence of Du Bois's interactions with the community is found in his engagements with the Atlanta chapter of the First Sociological Club. On at least one occasion he delivered a lecture to this body. Du Bois's 1897 lecture, "A Program for a Sociological Society," centered on six topical areas and championed the increased use of the sociological method by Blacks to improve their condition in the nation. The topical areas addressed in his speech included an explanation to attendees on what the discipline of sociology was, the articulation of what had been accomplished to date via sociology as a science, an explanation of the methods of research used for sociological inquiry, an explanation of how the data collected for sociological inquiry could be applied to a society, an articulation of what, in his opinion, had been the accomplishments of the First Sociological Club of Atlanta and an articulation of a vision for the organization's future endeavors. Additionally, while not much attention has historically been paid to Du Bois's civil rights activities, another example of his engagement with the community is found in his autobiography, where he explains, "I joined with the Negro leaders of Georgia in efforts to better local conditions; to stop discrimination in the distribution of school funds; and to keep the legislature from making further discrimination in railway travel" (Du Bois 1968: 219).

The fourth criterion of a school is that it must have as its key figure someone with a dominating personality. Included within this criterion is someone who demands the "personal loyalty and admiration of colleagues and students" (Bulmer 1985: 65) and who "look[s] for talented collaborators to participate in the research they conduct" (ibid.: 65–66). Upon assuming leadership of the research program in Atlanta Du Bois altered the direction of the studies, as discussed in Chapter 2, in a number of ways, including but not limited to, focusing on one specific topic per year and enhancing its scientific rigor. Du Bois (1968: 214) acknowledged that he "did not pause to consider how far my developed plans agreed or disagreed with the already launched project." Arguably, the primary reason for his lack of concern about how his plans for the studies would be received was his belief in the scientific inferiority of the ones conducted prior to his arrival. "As a scientific accomplishment," according to Du Bois ([1940] 1981: 1), "the first conference was not important." He believed the inaugural investigations were failures because they "followed the

Hampton and Tuskegee model of being primarily meetings of inspiration, directed toward specific efforts at social reform aimed at propaganda for social uplift in certain preconceived lines" (1968: 214). The firmness with which Du Bois managed the affairs of the investigations is also found in his interactions with colleagues and students.

Dorothy Yancy provides examples of his interactions with colleagues and students. According to Yancy (1978: 63–64) "colleagues had warm memories [of Du Bois] and called him the perfect host ... in a small group he was all right ... very warm. He was also witty in these small groups. He was known for proclaiming he 'got his Ph.D. when Ph.D.'s were Ph.D.'s.'" While his interactions with colleagues were often warm, Du Bois's students offered an alternative perspective. According to a former student, "Even though there was the intimacy of his suite and the small classes, many students felt he was aloof and an 'intellectual snob.' One student felt he was definitely not a 'hail fellow well met ... he was very gracious, [but had] a great deal of reserve. He laughed a lot, but even his laughter was reserved ... He made jokes, could see fun in things, but never a good horse laugh" (ibid.: 61).

The final component of this criterion is collaborative activities with colleagues. One of the biggest misnomers concerning the Atlanta Sociological Laboratory is the belief that Du Bois singularly collected every piece of data and wrote every report. As mentioned previously, because of financial limitations, this research unit, particularly in its early years, depended on the assistance of non-Atlanta University faculty, students and citizen researchers to collect data and write reports contained in many of the annual publications. Records from the Atlanta University publications cite the extensive participation and attendance of scholars and citizen researchers who assisted in data collection, made conference presentations or authored chapters. According to Du Bois (1968: 219), "In addition to the publications, we did something toward bringing together annually at Atlanta University persons and authorities interested in the problems of the South." The list of collaborators included well known scholars and activists like Jane Addams (Hull-House Settlement), Franz Boas (Columbia University), Florence Kelley (Hull-House Settlement), Kelly Miller (Howard University), Mary Church Terrell (Civil Rights Activist), Booker T. Washington (Tuskegee Institute), Max Weber, Walter Wilcox (United States Bureau of Labor and Commerce) and Richard R. Wright (University of Pennsylvania).

Foremost among the talented collaborators who assisted with research studies were Monroe Nathan Work and Lucy Craft Laney. Work, a sociologist at Booker T. Washington's Tuskegee Institute, published *The Negro Yearbook* for several years after the cessation of the Atlanta Sociological Laboratory. For a period of years Work's volumes at Tuskegee were the only source of accurate scholarly data on the condition of Blacks in America. As a graduate student at the University of Chicago, Work assisted with data collection for a number of

Atlanta University investigations. After taking the doctorate he continued to contribute to the research activities of the Atlanta Sociological Laboratory in at least three studies, as well as initiating his own research program at Tuskegee (Wright 2010).

Lucy Craft Laney is an exemplar of the participation of non-sociology trained citizen researchers who contributed to the annual investigations (Wright 2010). Laney, who in 1886 opened one of the first schools for Blacks in the state of Georgia, was an 1873 graduate of Atlanta University who embraced the opportunity to contribute to the body of scholarly knowledge on Blacks in America, especially in the South. She participated in at least five conferences as the presider over gender specific sessions covering women's issues and authored a number of sections in the annual publication. Her anecdotal contributions to discussions on the condition of Black women in the South foreshadowed the importance and significance of what Patricia Hill Collins would later call, 'taken-for-granted-knowledge.' According to Collins (2000: 34):

> The commonplace, taken-for-granted knowledge shared by African American women growing from our everyday thoughts and actions constitutes a first and most fundamental level of knowledge. The ideas that Black women share with one another on an informal, daily basis about topics such as how to style our hair, characteristics of 'good' Black men, strategies for dealing with White folks, and skills of how to 'get over' provide the foundations for this taken-for-granted knowledge.

While Lucy Craft Laney's contributions to the Atlanta University studies may not have been grounded in scholarly data, without question her theories on Black women's oppression in the United States were foundational and deeply rooted in the Black feminist intellectual tradition that would validate her contributions to the field nearly 100 years later.

The fifth criterion mandates that the leader possess an intellectual vision and have a missionary drive. Du Bois's intellectual vision and missionary drive are discussed in full in Chapter 2 and earlier in this chapter. Therefore, a full recounting of that information will not be offered here. However, a brief summary of Du Bois's vision and missionary drive is offered. Under the leadership of George G. Bradford the first two Atlanta University studies covered a wide range of topics and offered very little to the scientific understanding of life in America for its second class citizens. Du Bois immediately altered the direction of the investigations by focusing on one specific topic each year. By focusing on one topic per year the research laboratory could obtain a critical mass of data on that topic and construct resolutions (or theories) to address the problems discovered. Moreover, he divided the subjects into ten specific aspects of Black life and covered each over a ten year period. At the conclusion of the ten year period the same topic was revisited. This allowed Du Bois and his research team the opportunity to note changes that may have occurred in the ten year interval between investigations. Du Bois's utopian goal for his research program was the collection of 100 years of data on Blacks in America from which various theories on the *minority experience* could be developed. Reflecting on the possibilities missed concerning the Atlanta University studies, Du Bois (1968: 217) noted in his autobiography that:

> [The conference] did not stress enough the philosophy of Marx and Engels and was of course far too soon for Lenin. The program ought to have been— and as I think would have been if I had kept on this work—the Economic Development of the American Negro Slave; on this central thread all the other subjects would have been strung. But this I had no chance to essay.

Had Du Bois's plan for studying the social, economic and physical condition of Blacks in America continued longer it is quite possible that many of the social issues and concerns experienced by Blacks today would have been successfully addressed, and possibly ameliorated, years earlier.

The sixth criterion for a school states that there must be intellectual exchanges between colleagues and graduate students (e.g., the existence of seminars) and that the school must have an outlet for the publication of scholarship written by members of the school. This requirement is satisfied, as the yearly conference and publication of the Atlanta University Study of the Negro Problems served as the primary modes of intellectual exchange and publication outlet for the school. Concerning the intellectual exchanges between graduate students, this topic is addressed previously in this chapter as it was indicated that the sociological investigations of undergraduate and graduate students were included in a number of conferences and publications. Specifically, according to the 1897 Atlanta University catalog, undergraduate seminars in sociology were offered on statistics, general sociological principles and social and economic conditions, and a seminar in methods of reform was offered prior to the turn of the twentieth century (Atlanta University 1897). "In addition to this, graduate study of the social problems in the South by most approved scientific methods [was] carried on by the Atlanta Conference, composed of graduates of Atlanta, Fisk, and other institutions" (Atlanta University 1897: 13).

The seventh criterion mandates that a school have an adequate infrastructure. More precisely, this benchmark requires the school to accomplish advances in research methods, develop institutional links and have strong philanthropic support. The significant methodological contributions (e.g., the use of insider researchers, acknowledgement of the limitations of the research and triangulation) of this school are detailed earlier in this chapter and will not be repeated here. Institutional links are reflected in the participation of scholars and activists who were listed in the yearly publication as being contributors to the studies. This list includes, but is not limited to, Jane Addams (Hull-House Settlement), Franz Boas (Columbia University), James M. Colson (Virginia Normal & Collegiate Institute), Edward Cummings (Harvard University), John Hope (Atlanta Baptist College), Florence Kelley (Hull-House Settlement), Kelly Miller (Howard University), Mary Ovington (Greenpoint Settlement), Mary Church Terrell (Civil Rights Activist), Booker T. Washington (Tuskegee Institute) and Richard R. Wright (University of Pennsylvania).

The final component of this criterion is the garnering of strong philanthropic support. While Atlanta University did not garner philanthropic support matching that of the Rockefeller backed University of Chicago or the well-connected Tuskegee Institute of Booker T. Washington, that this school garnered funding to host nearly 30 conferences and publish 20 volumes of its research on issues of race and racism during an era in which Blacks could be killed for looking at or speaking to a White person in the wrong manner (as perceived by that White person) speaks volumes about its strong philanthropic support. Let us not forget that the state of Georgia withheld funds from the institution because of its non-discriminatory admissions policy, that some American philanthropic organizations were uninterested in funding research aimed directly at challenging their place in the American racial hierarchy and that funding was taken from the school because it embraced a liberal arts and not technical education curriculum. Even in the face of these challenges, the sociological research program at Atlanta University survived and, as best it could, thrived. Speaking of the difficulty of securing philanthropic support during this era, Du Bois ([1904] 1978: 55) argued:

> If the Negroes were still lost in the forests of central Africa we could have a government commission to go and measure their heads, but with 10 millions of them here under your noses I have in the past besought the Universities almost in vain to spend a single cent in a rational study of their characteristics and conditions … [A]t Atlanta University we beg annually and beg in vain for the paltry sum of $500 simply to aid us in replacing gross and vindictive ignorance of race conditions with enlightening knowledge and systematic observation.

This quote reflects Du Bois's frustration at the fact that he could not garner financial support of the levels enjoyed by Chicago or Tuskegee for the study of a group of people rising from the depths of slavery and marking the transition from rural to city life. The backing of such an endeavor, to Du Bois, would not benefit only the Black community; it would benefit the nation as a whole. Instead, Blacks were not viewed during this Jim Cow era as beings worthy of accurate and objective scientific inquiry in the minds of many Whites. As presented earlier, objective scientific studies from the medical and social science communities bolstered academic and laypersons' understandings of Blacks as a different type of human being and not necessarily worthy of extensive and truly objective study. Du Bois ([1904] 1978: 55) acknowledged this idea as he continued his commentary on the school's financial struggles.

> [I]f the Negroes are not ordinary human beings, if their development is simply the retrogression of an inferior people, and the only possible future for the Negro, a future of inferiority, decline and death, then it is manifest that a study of such a group, while still of interest and scientific value is of less pressing and immediate necessity than the study of a group which is distinctly recognized as belonging to the human family, whose advancement is possible, and whose future depends on its own efforts and the fairness and reasonableness of the dominant and surrounding group.

Although the institution was unable to garner philanthropic gifts matching those bestowed upon the University of Chicago, it was successful in obtaining external financial support for some studies. For example, funding was received from the Carnegie Institution for the 1907 study and the John F. Slater Fund provided support for studies conducted between 1908 and 1913. Elliott Rudwick (1974: 42) provides the most apropos statement on this topic when he writes:

> Since Atlanta University was a struggling and impoverished institution that could not afford to support Du Bois' research adequately for one year— much less for a decade or century—it is a tribute to his determination that he actually supervised the preparation of sixteen Atlanta University sociological monographs between 1897 and 1914.

Despite the difficulties encountered in amassing the financial support needed to carry out their studies, it is argued here that the fact that nearly 30 conferences were held and 20 monographs published are evidence of strong philanthropic support for the all-Black institution located in the heart of the Jim Crow American South, that pushed back against individual and institutional forces demanding that it conform to racist policies that were implemented at most institutions.

The eighth criterion indicates that a school cannot last beyond the generation of its central figure. By 1910 Du Bois realized that his presence on the faculty at Atlanta University negatively affected the school's philanthropic outreach efforts. Not wanting to continue hurting the university's fundraising efforts, he chose to resign from the faculty but remain director of the investigations in the hope that this tradeoff would rejuvenate funding for the school and spare the research program. In 1913 Du Bois relinquished his position as director of the Atlanta University Studies of the Negro Problems. After his complete departure from Atlanta University only two publications were released. One was an edited book of essays on the "race problem" and not original research. The other publication was an original research effort conducted by the school. Unfortunately, it did not mirror the quality of scientific rigor that Du Bois had established.

The ninth criterion of a school mandates that it be open to ideas and influences beyond its home discipline. Werner J. Lange argued that Du Bois's work was interdisciplinary at a time when such a practice was not common. According to Lange (1983: 143):

> It is important to note that Du Bois clearly delineated four approaches to 'the study of the Negro as a social group': (1) historical study; (2) statistical investigation; (3) anthropological measurement; and (4) sociological interpretation. The fact that these social scientific domains—now departmentally separated at most United States universities—constituted a single unit for Du Bois reflects the degree to which the young scholar valued and used a cross-disciplinary approach in his work. He was an accomplished historian, sociologist, statistician and anthropologist at a time when these disciplines were in their infancy in the United States.

Additionally, a cursory review of the titles of the 20 volumes of the Atlanta University studies provides evidence of interdisciplinarity as the subjects of the studies included business, crime and deviance, education, health and religion.

Chapter 4
Crashing thru the Gate(keepers)

Between 1895 and 1924 the Atlanta Sociological Laboratory led by W. E. B. Du Bois made significant contributions to the discipline of sociology. Its accomplishments include conducting one of the first objective scientific studies challenging racist theories on the physical and biological inferiority of Blacks, conducting the first sociological study on religion in the United States (Zuckerman 2000), becoming the first American sociological unit to institutionalize use of the insider researcher (Wright 2002a; 2002b), becoming the first American sociological unit to institutionalize the acknowledgement of the limitations of one's research (Wright 2002a; 2002b), becoming the first American sociological unit to institutionalize triangulation (Wright 2002a; 2002b) and establishing the first American school of sociology (Wright 2002a; 2002c). Had these feats been performed by White sociologists at a predominately White institution, it is not a stretch to suggest that the name of this school, its architects and their exploits would be engrained into the fiber of the American sociological enterprise to this day. A logical question that comes to mind is: Why *isn't* the Atlanta Sociological Laboratory engrained into the fabric of the mainstream sociological enterprise?

This question boggled my mind when I began researching this topic as a master's level student in the mid-1990s and remained in foreground of my thoughts as I completed doctoral training in 2000 with the Atlanta Sociological Laboratory as the subject of my dissertation. As I began my career as a professional sociologist I sought to articulate an academic answer to this question. Accordingly, I conducted a thorough examination of the existing literature. Despite the significant accomplishments of the Atlanta Sociological Laboratory, prior to Shaun L. Gabbidon's important 1999 article on Du Bois's contributions to the field of criminal justice that established him as a founder of that area, the sociological literature included only one entry on this school. Elliott Rudwick's article, "W. E. B. Du Bois and the Atlanta University Studies," assessed the Du Bois-led school's relevance and sociological significance. Rudwick concluded that Du Bois's research program deserved few accolades and little recognition within the sociological community because it suffered from considerable methodological weaknesses, lacked theoretical analysis and was mired in academic obscurity. Moreover, he argued that the school's impact on the discipline was largely negligible. According to Rudwick (1957: 475):

> The Atlanta Studies may not have improved the conditions of the race very much, but they probably did improve its morale. At a time when political and social restrictions upon the American Negroes were increasing, the Atlanta monographs must have provided many members of the race with a sense of group integration and ego satisfaction.

Using Rudwick's 1957 article as the foundation, I constructed five explanations for the more than 100-year marginalization of the Du Bois-led Atlanta University studies (Wright 2002b). My explanations of the sociological marginalization of the Atlanta Sociological Laboratory, the first three emanating from critiques offered by Rudwick, centered on 1) the idea that the methods of research were unsophisticated and of low quality; 2) the idea that the school excluded theoretical analysis; 3) the notion that the scholarly activities of the school were mired in academic obscurity; 4) the idea that the findings were ungeneralizable; and 5) racism. I will not provide an exhaustive review of each as this information can be found in more detail in article form elsewhere.[1] However, an overview is offered below.

Historical Exclusion from the Canon

Unsophisticated and Low Quality Methods of Research

The first explanation for the sociological marginalization of the Atlanta Sociological Laboratory rests on the idea that the methods of research employed by the school were unsophisticated and of low quality. This narrative is taken from Rudwick's 1957 article. In his critique of the Atlanta University studies Rudwick devoted most of his attention to what he perceived to be the methodological flaws of Du Bois's school. Rudwick (ibid.: 468) offered a general assessment of the school and suggested that "The Atlanta studies were of uneven quality in planning, structure, methods, and content." When discussing the first Du Bois-led Atlanta University study of 1898, Rudwick (ibid.: 469) argued that "[Du Bois] was not seriously troubled by the problem of sampling procedures … Nor did he have a passion for completeness." Offering a concluding thought on the flaws of the 1898 study Rudwick (ibid.:

---

1 See Earl Wright. 2002. "Why Black People Tend to Shout: An Earnest Attempt to Explain the Sociological Negation of the Atlanta Sociological Laboratory Despite Its Possible Unpleasantness." *Sociological Spectrum* 22(3): 325–361.

469) stated, "he provided no method for checking the reliability or validity of the material sent to him." While no substantive argument can be forged against the claims made by Rudwick concerning the 1898 study, it must be noted that Rudwick used the methodological failings of one study to make an argument against the entire 20 volumes of studies conducted. This strategy does not provide an accurate assessment of the methodological sophistication exercised during the tenure of the school. A full defense of the methodological sophistication of the Atlanta University studies is not presented here since this ground is covered in Chapter 3. However, it is interesting to note that Rudwick did not compare the methodological techniques used at Atlanta to those applied by any other sociological school that existed at the time; most notably, the Chicago School. Is it possible that Rudwick was aware of that school's challenges with methodological sophistication during the early twentieth century as discussed in Chapter 3? Or, was Rudwick simply viewing the works of a previous generation through a contemporary lens that colored all methodological techniques employed by early sociologists as antiquated? To judge the methodology of Atlanta, or Chicago for that matter, by today's standard is the essence of the phrase "hindsight is 20/20." Instead, the methodological contributions of the Atlanta Sociological Laboratory should be viewed through a lens similar to that of Francis L. Broderick (1959: 42), who asserted that "a later generation [of scholars] have doubts about [W. E. B. Du Bois's] methodology, for styles in scholarship change, and men see their grandfathers' ways as quaintly primitive." Viewed in this manner, the methodological contributions of the Atlanta Sociological Laboratory were massive and not a legitimate excuse for the marginalization of the school.

Lack of Theoretical Analysis

The second explanation of the sociological marginalization of the Atlanta Sociological Laboratory is the notion that it lacked theoretical analysis. This idea is taken from Rudwick who asserted that the school "lacked systematic theory" and Gabbidon (1999: 31) who argued that "[Du Bois] never stated any theoretical perspective that he later tested." These arguments fall short because, in the case of Gabbidon, it is not mandated that a theorist must test his or her creation in order for it qualify as a theoretical construct. Concerning Rudwick's argument, I propose that the Atlanta Sociological Laboratory *did* include theory. The resolutions presented in the conclusion of most Atlanta University publications comprised, when applicable, theoretical constructions. What I find problematic is the often ambiguous and discipline specific manner in which theoretical constructions are defined. I argue that the Atlanta Sociological Laboratory used a grounded theoretical approach to explain, predict and/or understand the findings gathered from the annual studies.

Perhaps the most troubling aspect of this discussion is the narrowly defined nature of theory. I borrow from my previous work to advance this argument:

> If one defines a theory as a set of interrelated statements that attempt to explain, predict or understand social events, and that can be replicated and generalizable, then the resolutions offered in the conclusion of the Atlanta University Conference Publications, after being tested by interested social scientists, qualify as systematic theoretical constructions. (Wright 2002b: 353)

It is without question that the form of theoretical analysis offered by Du Bois and the Atlanta Sociological Laboratory did not mirror that of its contemporaries. Notwithstanding this fact, an important but simple question remains: "Despite its difference in presentation from standard sociological theories, should Atlanta University's theoretical contributions be minimized because, although they qualify for theoretical status according to a strict definition of the term, they do not qualify ideologically" (ibid.: 354)? The answer to this question is, no.

Academic Obscurity

The third explanation for the Atlanta school's sociological marginalization is the idea that its works were hidden in academic obscurity. This notion is derived from Rudwick's (1957: 475) critique where he argued that, "Du Bois's studies never gained any wide circulation ... [although] reviews of them appeared in important magazines and in some metropolitan newspapers." Although Rudwick seemingly contradicts his own argument, the idea that the works produced by Du Bois and his Atlanta colleagues were mired in academic obscurity is debunked after one reviews the Atlanta University publications and learns that the school listed the names of persons from whom copies of the previous year's study were requested and to whom they were delivered. For example, copies of the studies were delivered to undergraduate and graduate students at schools including, but not limited to, Harvard University, the University of Texas and Wellesley College. In fact, one North Carolina high school requested and received a copy of an early study on education. Additionally, copies were sent to organizations including, but not limited to, the United States Bureau of Labor, *The New York Independent* and *McClure's Magazine*. Lectures on the findings of some studies were delivered by Atlanta University researchers to social science clubs in cities around the nation.

It is quite possible that Rudwick may have been referring to mainstream White sociologists when he referenced the Atlanta school's lack of *wide circulation*. If this is the case then that point is also debunked. For example, according to Du Bois (1968: 218):

> Professor E. R. A. Seligman, [professor of Economics at Columbia University] wrote: 'I take great pleasure in testifying to my very high appreciation of the studies on the Negro problem that you have been editing for the past few years. They are essentially scholarly and that means sober and temperate, and they are covering a field which is almost untilled and which is not apt to be cultivated by others.'

Du Bois added that "Jane Addams attended our conference in 1908 and commended our work" (ibid.: 218). Howard Odum (1951: 378), in a book on the history of the discipline up to 1950, acknowledged his familiarity with the significance of the Atlanta University studies when he wrote that Du Bois was the "originator and editor of the pioneering *Atlanta Sociological Studies* from 1897 to 1910." Conclusively, the idea that the sociological activity of the Atlanta Sociological Laboratory was shrouded in secrecy is a misnomer and should not be considered a legitimate explanation for the schools marginalization.

Ungeneralizable Findings

The fourth explanation of the Atlanta school's sociological marginalization is the idea that its findings were ungeneralizable. It is true that not every Atlanta University study published during the school's 20-year run produced findings that were generalizable to the entire population. It is also true that a number of the studies did produce data that were generalizable to specific members of the American population, Blacks in the American South and Black males. Moreover, it is worth noting that a primary objective of the founders of the Atlanta research program was to produce findings that were generalizable beyond Blacks, when possible. President Bumstead acknowledged this at the inaugural 1896 conference:

> The general subject of this and succeeding conferences—the study of Negro city life—and the subject of this year—the morality of Negroes in Cities— constitute a human problem far more than a Negro problem. We shall use the words 'Negro' and 'colored,' not to emphasize distinctions of race, but as terms of convenience. We are simply to study human life under certain conditions—conditions which, if repeated with any other race, would have practically the same result … The improvement of Negro life anywhere will

be a blessing to the life of the nation as a whole, regardless of race or color. (Atlanta University 1896: 6–7)

The 1897 study examined the "Social and Physical Condition of Negroes in Cities" and serves as an example of a study that could have been generalized to the larger American population. In this investigation it was discovered that many Black urban residents employed unsanitary hygiene practices and often ignored common conventions regarding their health. The lack of proper sanitation practice was not exclusive to Blacks. Accordingly, resolutions such as this one were applicable beyond race. Additionally, it was concluded in this study that the high rate of consumption (now called tuberculosis) for Blacks was caused by a lack of ventilation in many urban buildings. Since Blacks were not the only people living in poorly ventilated housing in urban American areas, it stands to reason that this conclusion drawn by Atlanta researchers could also be applied beyond Blacks to White and European ethnic groups living in urban cities and experiencing similar conditions.

The 1906 investigation, "Health and Physique of the Negro American," was one of the earliest scientific investigations to debunk the scientific racism theories of the early twentieth century, which promoted the idea of the biological and physical inferiority of Blacks vis-à-vis Whites. Using a sample of 1,000 Hampton University students, Atlanta University researchers examined their physical characteristics and used that data comparatively against those of Whites to conclude that their existed no substantive differences between the physical make-up of the two races. This conclusion did not simply apply to Blacks in the greater Virginia area or the southern United States; this finding was applicable to all Blacks in America.

The 1904 study, "Some Notes on Negro Crime Particularly in Georgia," produced findings that were generalizable to Blacks living in the southern United States, in general, and Black males, specifically. Although slavery was ruled unconstitutional with the passage of the Thirteenth Amendment to the U. S. Constitution, the form of pseudo slavery known as convict leasing, whereby imprisoned Black males (though not exclusively males) were leased out for labor, often having been convicted for minor violations or on falsified testimony of Whites, was birthed shortly thereafter. According to Atlanta University researchers, "The state became a dealer in crime, profited by it so as to derive a net annual income from her prisoners. The lessees of convicts made large profits also" (Du Bois 1904: 5). This proved to be a moneymaking endeavor for southern states as it was the only region in the nation to garner a profit on this practice. Moreover, this practice proved to be more impactful on Blacks, specifically Black males, than Whites or any other group. "If the criminal were white, public opinion refused to permit him to enter the [convict lease program] save in the most extreme cases" (ibid.: 5). "On the other hand, so customary had it become to convict any Negro upon a mere accusation, that public opinion was loathe to allow a fair trial to black suspects, and was too often tempted to take the law into its own hands" (ibid.: 5). Thus, Black males in the American South were vulnerable to becoming clogs within the neo-slavery machine that existed post emancipation. Although the Atlanta Sociological Laboratory may not have produced generalizable findings by the standards applied by social scientists of today, it is without question that many of the findings of the school were generalizable to populations beyond Blacks.

Racism

Explanations of the sociological marginalization of the Atlanta Sociological Laboratory presented to this point include the ideas that the school suffered from low quality and unsophisticated methods of research, lacked theoretical analysis, was mired in academic obscurity and that its findings were ungeneralizable. Neither singly nor cumulatively do the explanations offered above satisfactorily answer the question of why the Du Bois-led Atlanta Sociological Laboratory was sociologically marginalized and rendered invisible. Notwithstanding the explanations offered previously, I argue that the primary cause of the school's historical marginalization and invisibility is racism: individual and institutional.

The idea that the accomplishments of non-White male sociologists have been largely excluded from the historical record in conversations on significant contributors to the discipline is supported by Barbara Peters (1991: 248–249), who argued that since "the founding of the first academic department at the University of Chicago ... [S]ociology has had a history of silencing voices that were different from the dominant White, male, bourgeois, and 'moral' voices of the founding 'fathers.'" The silencing of the contributions of Du Bois and the Atlanta Sociological Laboratory stems, in part, from the ways that race was *lived* and *experienced* in the late 1800s and early 1900s. This idea is best captured using Karl Mannheim's sociology of knowledge as a framework of understanding.

Mannheim's sociology of knowledge perspective allows for an understanding of events, past and present, through a lens that takes into account social location and societal environment in specific places and at specific times. If we are able to ascertain the intersectional operation of social location and societal factors on a people's understanding of their (then) current world events then, I argue, a better understanding of their actions can be articulated. Stated another way, if we can understand that the racial milieu, for example, of pre modern Civil Rights America considered it anathema that a non-White person could make substantive contributions to the discipline of sociology, then the historical exclusion of the Du Bois-led Atlanta Sociological Laboratory can be understood even in its ugliness. Mannheim (1968: 238) argued that his perspective "does not refer only to specific assertions which may be regarded as concealment, falsifications or lies," but "examines [these issues] on structural, [cultural, and/or ideological] level[s], which it views as not being the same for all men, but rather as allowing the same subject to take on different forms and aspects in the course of social development." Thus, if the Atlanta Sociological Laboratory existed, as mentioned in Chapter 3, in a racial milieu where scientific data *proved* that Blacks were intellectually and physically inferior to Whites, how, then, could the mainstream sociological community recognize, embrace and canonize the works of those who, by many of their own writings, were considered inferior? The answer is simple. They did not. The idea that Blacks in America could make substantive contributions to the country, in general, and to the discipline, specifically, was not a belief that was embraced by an overwhelming majority of Americans at the turn of the twentieth century. Moreover, it is ironic that the seminal works conducted at Atlanta University were taking place in this racialized environment as the discipline's canonization process was starting.

Instead of promoting the best sociological works of the era, regardless of race, the flagship publication of the discipline, *American Journal of Sociology*, provided aid and comfort to the existing scientific racism theories of the day. According to Rudwick (1974: 47):

> Despite the depth of Du Bois's commitment to sociology, he was in the main ignored by the elite in the profession. It is interesting to note that Albion W. Small, a founder of America's first department of sociology in 1892, of the *American Journal of Sociology* in 1895, and of the American Sociological Society a decade later, had, like Du Bois, been trained in Germany by Schmoller ... In spite of this similarity in professional background and although the *American Journal of Sociology* ... devoted many pages to social welfare problems, Small clearly considered Du Bois's work of minor importance [because of his relative omission of Du Bois's works at Atlanta University].

Instead, according to Rudwick (ibid.: 47):

> [B]ooks by known racists were reviewed and often warmly praised. In 1906, Thomas Nelson Page's *The Negro: The Southerner's Problem* was glowingly lauded by Charles Ellwood, who had been Small's graduate student ... In another review, Ellwood gratitiously commented, "it is only through the full recognition that the average Negro is still a savage child of nature that the North and South can be brought to unite in work to uplift the race."

It would be neither accurate nor fair to suggest that all of the writings included in the *American Journal of Sociology* supported the scientific racism theories of the era. Rudwick (ibid.: 48) argued:

> It is true that the *Journal* did carry articles by a man like W. I. Thomas, who criticized racist theories, but other items displayed the racial biases of their authors. The September 1903 issue included an article by H. E. Berlin entitled 'The Civil War as Seen through Southern Glasses,' in which the author described slavery as 'the most humane and the most practical method ever devised for "bearing the white man's burden."' The publication of such views in the *American Journal of Sociology* reflected theories about race held in the profession at the time.

Dan S. Green and Edwin Driver (1976: 331) provide a concluding statement on the racial milieu within the discipline during the early twentieth century when they wrote:

> [R. Charles] Key's analysis of the writings of Sumner, Giddings, Small, Ward and Ross, [the Big 5 presidents of the American Sociological Association between 1905 and 1914], leads him to conclude [that] … The racism of the pioneer sociologists and the incidents of racism found in their works seem to range from unashamed bigotry to tacit acceptance. Their racism can be understood in the same manner by which their theories and prophecies can be understood; with reference to the socio-culture in which they took meaning and shape; their opportunity structures, 'styles of life,' and world views.

It was within this American racial climate that the tremendous works and accomplishments of the Atlanta Sociological Laboratory were ignored and sentenced to disciplinary purgatory for more than 100 years. It wasn't until the late 1990s that Shaun L. Gabbidon and I began to force academia to take seriously the significance of the Atlanta Sociological Laboratory to sociology specifically and the social sciences in general, via our publication of articles and books. Now that the exploits of this school have been presented to a broad audience through this book a final question remains: Where do we go from here?

Inserting the Atlanta Sociological Laboratory into the Canon

In the previous chapters the origin, significant contributions and sociological marginalization of the Atlanta Sociological Laboratory have been presented.

This endeavor concludes with a few recommendations on how this school can be infused into the American sociological canon.

Integration into the Sociology Curriculum

Over the past 20 years there has been an increase in the diverse representations of early contributors to the discipline in introductory sociology textbooks. Harriet Martineau, Ida B. Wells, Jane Addams and W. E. B. Du Bois are all mentioned, in some fashion, in most of the leading textbooks. When Du Bois is highlighted his work receives, generally, a paragraph or so wherein recognition of his accomplishments at the Atlanta Sociological Laboratory are never discussed. Instead, emphasis is placed on *The Philadelphia Negro*, concepts including double consciousness and talented tenth and his ideological sparring with Booker T. Washington. When Atlanta University is mentioned it is usually as an addendum to note that his years as a practicing sociologist took place at the institution (Wright 2014). No discussion of the school's sociological contributions is presented or acknowledged. Given the massive sociological accomplishments identified in this book, it is unquestionable that the Atlanta Sociological Laboratory should be featured prominently in, at a minimum, introduction to sociology textbooks and course readings in relevant substantive topical areas.

The Atlanta Sociological Laboratory can be easily integrated into introductory sociology courses. The infusion of this school into the curriculum can begin with discussions on the history of the discipline and its development in America. While the University of Kansas established the first department with sociology in its title, the Department of History and Sociology, and the University of Chicago established the first department with sociology as its singular department name, Atlanta University fits within the discussion on early American sociology as the school established its department only a few years after Chicago. Within this section, wherein Atlanta University's status as having established one of the first departments of sociology is discussed, a teaser of the school's methodological accomplishments can be introduced. A more thorough examination of the school's methodological contributions can be presented during the lecture and discussion on research methods. In addition to these areas, Du Bois and the school's significance to the area of religion, for example, can be presented when covering that topical area.

Phil Zuckerman argues that, although Émile Durkheim, Max Weber and Charlotte Perkins Gilman all penned respected monographs, Du Bois's 1903 Atlanta University study on religion should be recognized as the first sociological offering on the topic in the United States. Zuckerman (2000: 242) writes: "It is important to note that Du Bois' contemporaries (and recognized founders of the sociology of religion), while offering brilliant insights, did so without a similar resonance [as Du Bois] upon what today would constitute standard sociological research methods." "Du Bois' emphasis," according to Zuckerman (ibid.: 242), "upon empirically driven research is clearly evidenced in his study of religion: he got involved in the religious life that surrounded him to a degree unparalleled by other scholars of his day." Zuckerman (ibid.: 250) concludes that Du Bois:

> should be regarded as the first American sociologist of religion ... [because] he employed standard sociological research methods to a degree unparalleled by the canonized classical sociologists of religion ... [and because his research] stressed the ways in which religious institutions can be recognized as social, communal centers which provide this worldly rewards and comforts.

Du Bois's Atlanta work can also be infused into the topical area of race and ethnicity. However, it cannot be overstated that the works of this school should not be ghettoized into the singular space of sociology of race and ethnicity. Yes, the Atlanta Sociological Laboratory's principal sample consisted of American Blacks. However, many of its findings, significant outcomes and sociological advances extend far beyond the realm of race. It is imperative that the school not be held captive to the narrow lens whereby it is viewed as significant only to those studying race and ethnicity. Instead, the accomplishments of this school, while grounded in the notion of race, are expansive, broad and can be infused into a variety of areas including, but not limited to, crime and deviance, education, research methods, family, religion, sociology of the South and urban sociology.

The infusion of Du Bois's Atlanta Sociological Laboratory into the sociology curriculum should include graduate instruction as well. Specifically, all American sociology doctoral programs are challenged to infuse the seminal works of the Atlanta Sociological Laboratory into, at a minimum, their theory and research methods courses as its works are as foundational as those of any scholar or school currently studied. Moreover, doctoral programs that list as their areas of departmental excellence crime and deviance, education, family, race and ethnicity, religion and urban sociology are especially challenged to infuse the scholarship of the Atlanta Sociological Laboratory into their curriculums, since to not do so would be a purposeful disservice to their students if a goal of their program is to expose them to the highest forms of sociological research and training, both past and present. By infusing the Atlanta Sociological Laboratory into the sociology curriculum the instructors and institutions will serve as active allies of the school and signal to the mainstream academic community that they embrace a new and holistic understanding of the significance and contributions of scholars and units who have heretofore been excluded from serious sociological examination and canonization.

Citation Respect

One of the measures often used to determine the significance and relevance of one's work is the number of times it is cited by others. For many of us this is one of the measures used, whether explicitly or implicitly, to determine whether or not we are granted tenure and/or promotion. As it relates to works considered classic and those canonized in the discipline, it would be considered anathema not to cite or note, for example, August Comte when discussing the origin of the discipline, Karl Marx when discussing economics and oppression or Émile Durkheim when discussing macro level societal structures. In the same manner, it should be abhorrent to have scholars write on the subjects identified herein and not cite the scholarship of the Atlanta Sociological Laboratory. Again, I want to stress that the accomplishments of this school extend beyond the area of race and ethnicity as it should not be ghettoized into that singular frame. Instead, these works should be cited in areas including, but not limited to, crime and deviance, education, research methods, family, religion, sociology of the South and urban sociology.

Become an Advocate

An ally is someone who joins an effort to provide support to a cause. Instructors who infuse the works of the Du Bois-led Atlanta Sociological Laboratory into their curriculum are allies of the school. Advocates, on the other hand, are those who argue for and provide support for a cause. Whereas allies offer support, possibly tacitly, advocates are active in promoting a specific cause. What is proposed here is the establishment of a critical mass of advocates of the Atlanta Sociological Laboratory. The significance of having advocates in the discipline of sociology is addressed by Platt who implicitly suggests that Du Bois, and by extension the Atlanta Sociological Laboratory, were allowed to fall into mainstream academic obscurity for nearly 100 years because of racism, and more germane here, a lack of advocates. Platt (1996: 247) proposes that despite his tremendous pedigree and scholarly accomplishments, "he was Black, and his race meant that he could not hope for a job in a [White] research university; thus he could not have the opportunity to train research students who would carry his legacy to the mainstream of white sociology." As discussed earlier, Du Bois did train graduate students at Atlanta University. However, the training of master's level graduate students at Atlanta University with little to no opportunity or desire to pursue doctoral work left Du Bois and his school in the position in which the critical mass of advocates to carry on the legacy of the school was nil. One need to only look at the many graduates of the master's and doctoral programs at the University of Chicago and their voluminous works on the history, faculty and contributions of the school to understand the importance of having institutional advocates. Platt (ibid.: 248) further emphasizes the significance of advocates in stating, "The writer who leaves a surviving entourage with a stake in the continuity of the original reputation is more likely to have steps taken which enhance memory." In lieu of the Atlanta Sociological Laboratory not having such an entourage, I propose that a number of entities should serve as advocates for the first American school of sociology.

The preponderance of the responsibility for promoting and advancing the legacy of the W. E. B. Du Bois-led Atlanta Sociological Laboratory rests on the shoulders of those who consider themselves Du Bois scholars but rarely, if ever, cite his accomplishments made at the school. Similar to the critique offered on introductory sociology textbooks, the number of books and articles written about Du Bois that either ignore or provide cursory attention to his years at Atlanta University is astounding. If any group should bear the primary responsibility of advocating for the mainstream recognition of the achievements of the Atlanta Sociological Laboratory it is this group.

Second, departments of sociology that pride themselves on being promoters of justice, equality, fairness and inclusion are called upon to become advocates of the Du Bois-led research program, especially if your program is in the American South. There are a number of departments of sociology that, at least tacitly, advertise their openness to and provide instruction in non-traditional theory, methods and substantive topical areas. These departments that embrace robust expansions of their curriculums on the contributions of women and members of the LGBTQ community are challenged to also embrace the works of this school of similarly marginalized sociology scholars in an effort to make the discipline more holistic. Doctoral programs in the South, and especially those in the state of Georgia, are challenged to serve as advocates of the Atlanta Sociological Laboratory. Outside of the narrow and regionally specific accolades offered to Howard W. Odum and the University of North Carolina, departments of sociology in the southern region of the United States receive little to no recognition for their historical contributions to the discipline. While it would seem awkward for an institution to prominently feature and laud the accomplishments of another school in its program (although, this seems to have never been a major issue as it relates to the mainstream acceptance and promotion of the Chicago School of Sociology), such a task can be framed as recognition of the type of subject matter and scholarship that can be accomplished at a similarly situated southern institution. This task can be performed easily at the leading institutions in the state of Georgia.

Last, I call upon Howard University to be a strong advocate for the Atlanta Sociological Laboratory. This challenge is offered for three reasons. First, when Du Bois restarted the second era of studies, the Phylon Institute, its life span at Atlanta University was cut short because of Du Bois's forced retirement. The second era of studies did not immediately end with Du Bois's retirement. Sociologists at Howard University embraced the challenge of carrying on Du Bois's work. Although the attempt was not successful, that Howard embraced the challenge signaled its willingness to continue a tradition it believed to be valuable within the substantive area of Black sociology. Second, the Howard University community has a long history of participating in the Atlanta University studies. Whether through student participation or research reports by faculty including W. Montague Cobb and Kelly Miller, Howard has always embraced the mission and goals of the Atlanta sociological research program in sociology and advocacy of the school via its graduate curriculum would be the next stage of that collaboration. The final reason that I call upon Howard University to be an advocate of the Atlanta Sociological Laboratory is because it is the only Historically Black College or University (HBCU) in the nation with a doctoral program in sociology. As the only doctoral program at an HBCU, Howard is specially situated to provide a holistic program of sociological inquiry to its students. Moreover, the school can become a leader in re-designing for the nation our understanding of the early contributors to the discipline, within and beyond the area of race, through robust examinations of, for example, early Black female sociologists and social scientists including Lucy Laney, Ida B. Wells-Barnett and Maria Stewart. Such an agenda would place Howard at the forefront of a new re-articulation of an updated and revised doctoral curriculum—a curriculum through which students are taught using the best exemplars of sociological excellence conducted in the United States, and not simply a curriculum and canon that has been passed along from generation to generation without question or regard to new discoveries within the field.

Conclusion

For more than 120 years the sociological accomplishments of the W. E. B. Du Bois-led Atlanta Sociological Laboratory have been ignored by mainstream sociologists. The contributions of this school include being the first American sociological unit to institutionalize the acknowledgement of the limitations of one's research, the first American sociological unit to institutionalize use of the insider researcher, the first American sociological unit to institutionalize method triangulation and establishing itself as the first American school of sociology. If these accomplishments had been performed by White sociologists at a predominately White institution it is without question that each and every person trained in sociology or who ever took a course in the discipline would have, at a minimum, been introduced to some aspect of its greatness. For the scholarly contributions of this school to not be readily known, canonized and taught in every department of sociology in this nation is a travesty and scandal that *must* be rectified. The impetus for this book was to insure that a baseline of information on this school was available so that it might be used to infuse this material into the sociology curriculum. It is my hope, 120 years after the first conference and release of its first publication, that the W. E. B. Du Bois-led Atlanta Sociological Laboratory may finally receive its deserved vaunted status in the discipline, for its scholarship represents some of the most seminal contributions to the discipline. If this school does not become a part of the American canon of classic works in sociology then Du Bois's (1968: 228) poignant words concerning race and the legacy of Blacks and their scholarship will continue to ring true.

So far as the American world of science and letters was concerned, we never 'belonged;' we remained unrecognized in learned societies and academic groups. We rated merely as Negroes studying Negroes, and after all, what had Negroes to do with America or science?

Bibliography

Adams, Myron W. 1930. *A History of Atlanta University*. Atlanta: Atlanta University Press.

Atlanta University. 1896. *Mortality among Negroes in Cities: The Atlanta University Publications, No. 1*. Atlanta: Atlanta University Press.

Atlanta University. 1897. *Social and Physical Condition of Negroes in Cities: The Atlanta University Publications, No. 2*. Atlanta: Atlanta University Press.

Atlanta University. 1897. *Catalogue of the Officers and Students of Atlanta University (Incorporated 1867–Opened 1869)*. Atlanta: Atlanta University Press.

Atlanta University. 1899. *Catalogue of the Officers and Students of Atlanta University (Incorporated 1867–Opened 1869)*. Atlanta: Atlanta University Press.

Beard, Augustus F. 1909. *A Crusade of Brotherhood: A History of the American Missionary Association*. Boston: The Pilgrim Press.

Berg, Bruce L. 2004. *Qualitative Research Methods for the Social Sciences*. New York: Allyn and Bacon.

Bernard, Luther L. 1918. "The Teaching of Sociology in Southern Colleges and Universities." *American Journal of Sociology* 23(4): 491–515.

Bernard, Luther L. 1948. "Sociological Trends in the South." *Social Forces* 27(1): 12–19.

Bigham, J. A. 1915. *Select Discussions of Race Problems: The Atlanta University Publications, No. 20*. Atlanta: Atlanta University Press.

Blyden, Edward W. 1887. *Christianity, Islam and the Negro Race*. London: W. B. Whittingham.

Bowles, Frank and Frank DeCosta. 1971. *Between Two Worlds: A Profile of Negro Higher Education*. New York: McGraw-Hill.

Broderick, Francis L. 1959. *W. E. B. Du Bois: Negro Leader in a Time of Crisis*. Stanford, CA: Stanford University Press.

Brown, Thomas I. 1917. *Economic Co-operation among the Negroes of Georgia: The Atlanta University Publications, No. 19*. Atlanta: Atlanta University Press.

Bulmer, Martin. 1984. *The Chicago School of Sociology: Institutionalization, Diversity, and the Rise of Sociological Research*. Chicago: University of Chicago Press.

——— . 1985. "The Chicago School of Sociology: What Made It a School." *History of Sociology* 5(2): 61–77.

Bumstead, Horace, [1918] 1981. Letter from Horace Bumstead to James Weldon Johnson, February 22, 1918. W. E. B. Du Bois Papers. Special Collections and University Archives, University of Massachusetts Amherst Libraries.

Byrd, W. Michael and Linda A. Clayton. 2001. "Race, Medicine, and Health Care in the United States: A Historical Survey. *Journal of the National Medical Association* 93(3 Supplement): 11S–34S.

Collins, Patricia H. 1991. "Learning From the Outsider Within: The Sociological Significance of Black Feminist Thought." pp. 35–59 in *Beyond Methodology: Feminist Research as Lived Scholarship*, edited by Mary Margaret Fonow and Judith A. Cook. Bloomington, IN: Indiana University Press.

Comas, Juan. 1961. "'Scientific' Racism Again." *Current Anthropology* 2(4): 303–340.

Dennis, Rutledge M. 1975. "The Sociology of W. E. B. Du Bois." Ph.D. dissertation, Washington State University, Pullman, WA.

Du Bois, William Edward Burghardt. 1898. *Some Efforts of American Negroes for Their Own Social Betterment: The Atlanta University Publications, No. 3*. Atlanta: Atlanta University Press.

——— . 1899. *The Negro in Business: The Atlanta University Publications, No. 4*. Atlanta: Atlanta University Press.

——— . 1900. *The College-Bred Negro: The Atlanta University Publications, No. 5*. Atlanta: Atlanta University Press.

——— . 1901. *The Negro Common School: The Atlanta University Publications, No. 6*. Atlanta: Atlanta University Press.

——— . 1902. *The Negro Artisan: The Atlanta University Publications, No. 7*. Atlanta: Atlanta University Press.

——— . 1903a. *The Negro Church: The Atlanta University Publications, No. 8*. Atlanta: Atlanta University Press.

——— . [1903] 1978. "The Laboratory in Sociology at Atlanta University." pp. 61–69 in *W. E. B. Du Bois on Sociology and the Black Community*, edited by Dan S. Green and Edwin D. Driver. Chicago: University of Chicago Press.

——— . 1904. *Some Notes on Negro Crime in Georgia: The Atlanta University Publications, No. 9*. Atlanta: Atlanta University Press.

——— . [1904b] 1978. "The Atlanta Conferences." pp. 53–60 in *W. E. B. Du Bois on Sociology and the Black Community*, edited by Dan S. Green and Edwin D. Driver. Chicago: University of Chicago Press.

——— . 1905. *A Select Bibliography of the American Negro: The Atlanta University Publications, No. 10*. Atlanta: Atlanta University Press.

——— . 1906. *The Health and Physique of the Negro American: The Atlanta University Publications, No. 11*. Atlanta: Atlanta University Press.

——— . 1907. *Economic Co-operation Among Negro Americans: The Atlanta University Publications, No. 12*. Atlanta: Atlanta University Press.

——— . 1908. *The Negro American Family: The Atlanta University Publications, No. 13*. Atlanta: Atlanta University Press.

——— . 1909. *Efforts for Social Betterment among Negro Americans: The Atlanta University Publications, No. 14*. Atlanta: Atlanta University Press.

———. [1940] 1981. "The Atlanta University Studies of Social Conditions among Negroes: 1896–1913." W. E. B. Du Bois Papers. Special Collections and University Archives, University of Massachusetts Amherst Libraries.

———. [1940] 1968. *Dusk of Dawn: An Essay Toward An Autobiography of a Race Concept.* New York: Schocken Books.

———. 1940. "Apology." *Phylon* 1(1): 3–5.

———. [1960] 1981. "The Scientific Study of the American Negro." W. E. B. Du Bois Papers. Special Collections and University Archives, University of Massachusetts, Amherst Libraries.

———. 1961. W. E. B. Du Bois: A Recorded Biography (Interviewed by Moses Asch). Folkways Records and Service Corporation: New York.

———. 1968. *The Autobiography of W. E. B. Du Bois: A Soliloquy on Viewing My Life from the Last Decade of Its First Century.* New York: International Publishers.

Du Bois, W. E. B. and Augustus Granville Dill. 1910. *The College-Bred Negro American: The Atlanta University Publications, No. 15.* Atlanta: Atlanta University Press.

———. 1911. *The Common School and the American Negro: The Atlanta University Publications, No. 16.* Atlanta: Atlanta University Press.

———. 1912. *The Negro American Artisan: The Atlanta University Publications, No. 17.* Atlanta: Atlanta University Press.

———. 1913. *Morals and Manners among Negro Americans: The Atlanta University Publications, No. 18.* Atlanta: Atlanta University Press.

Gabbidon, Shaun L. 1999. "W. E. B. Du Bois and the 'Atlanta School' of Social Scientific Research, 1897–1913." *Journal of Criminal Justice Education* 10(1): 21-38.

Green, Dan S. and Edwin D. Driver. 1976. "W. E. B. Du Bois: A Case in the Sociology of Sociological Negation." *Phylon* 37: 308–333.

Hammersley, Martyn. 1989. *The Dilemma of Qualitative Method: Herbert Blumer and the Chicago Tradition.* New York: Routledge Press.

Hunter, Frances L. 1922. "Slave Society on the Southern Plantation." *Journal of Negro History* 7(1): 1–10.

Irvine, Russell W. 2001. "Coming South: The Reverend John Howard Hincks, A Five-Year (1889–1994) Window in the Development of Atlanta University and the Social Sciences." *Phylon* 49: 229–265.

Lange, Werner J. 1983. "W. E. B. Du Bois and the First Scientific Study of Afro-America." *Phylon* 44: 135–146.

Mannheim, Karl. 1968. *Ideology and Utopia: An Introduction to the Sociology of Knowledge.* New York: Harcourt, Brace, & World, Inc.

Odum, Howard W. 1951. *American Sociology: The Story of Sociology in the United States through 1950.* London: Greenwood.

Peters, Barbara J. 1991. "Disparate Voices: The Magic Show of Sociology." *American Sociologist* 22: 246–260.

Platt, Jennifer. 1987. "The Chicago School and Firsthand Data." Paper given at the annual conference of CHEIRON (The European Society for the History of Behavioural and Social Sciences).

Platt, Jennifer. 1996. *A History of Sociological Research Methods in America, 1920–1960*. Cambridge: Cambridge University Press.

Rudwick, Elliott M. 1957. "W. E. B. Du Bois and the Atlanta University Studies on the Negro." *Journal of Negro Education* 26: 466–476.

Rudwick, Elliott M. 1974. "W. E. B. Du Bois as Sociologist." pp. 25–55 in *Black Sociologists: Historical and Contemporary Perspectives*, edited by James E. Blackwell and Morris Janowitz. Chicago: University of Chicago Press.

Wilcox, Walter. 1904. *Negroes in the United States*. Department of Commerce and Labor, Bureau of the Census, Washington D.C.: Government Printing Office, United States.

Wright II, Earl. 2012. "Why, Where and How to Infuse the Atlanta Sociological Laboratory into the Sociology Curriculum." *Teaching Sociology* 40: 257–270.

Wright II, Earl. 2009. "Beyond W. E. B. Du Bois: A Note on Some of the Lesser Known Members of the Atlanta Sociological Laboratory" *Sociological Spectrum* 29(6): 700–717.

Wright II, Earl. 2006. "W. E. B. Du Bois and the Atlanta University Studies on the Negro, *Revisited*." *Journal of African American Studies* 9(4): 3–17.

Wright II, Earl. 2002. "The Atlanta Sociological Laboratory, 1896–1924: A Historical Account of the First American School of Sociology." *Western Journal of Black Studies* 26(3): 165–174.

Wright II, Earl. 2002. "Why Black People Tend To Shout!: An Earnest Attempt To Explain the Sociological Negation of the Atlanta Sociological Laboratory Despite Its Possible Unpleasantness." *Sociological Spectrum* 22(3): 325–361.

Wright II, Earl. 2002. "Using The Master's Tools: Atlanta University and American Sociology, 1896–1924." *Sociological Spectrum* 22(1): 15–39.

Wright II, Earl and Thomas C. Calhoun. 2006. "Jim Crow Sociology: Toward An Understanding of the Origin and Principles of Black Sociology via the Atlanta Sociological Laboratory." *Sociological Focus* 39(1): 1–18.

Yancy, Dorothy C. 1978. "William Edward Burghardt Du Bois' Atlanta Years: The Human Side—A Study Based Upon Oral Sources." *Journal of Negro History* 63: 59–67.

Zuckerman, Phil. 2000. *Du Bois on Religion*. Oxford: Rowman & Littlefield.

Index